Totally Awesome Training
Activity Guide

Aimee -

amazing!

Gloria

Totally Awesome Training Activity Guide

50+ Small Business Training Activities that Work!

Monica Cornetti

www.entreprenowonline.com

ISBN 978-0-9789229-5-5

Editor: *Jonathan Peters*
Interior Design and Layout: *Joe Cornetti*
Content Assistants: *Lou Cornetti and Lindsey Rock*   3

Second Edition
© 2013 by Monica Cornetti
All rights reserved.

First Edition, © 2008 by Monica Cornetti

Published by EntrepreNow! Press
Plano, TX

ISBN 978-0-9789229-5-5
Printed in the United States of America

www.entreprenowonline.com

CONTENTS

ACKNOWLEDGEMENTS

While working with entrepreneurs and small business owners in the start and growth of their business, I am always thrilled and excited when a training session helps them solve their business challenges. Watching them grasp the content of the training through activities, interaction with other seminar participants and self-reflection, is an intensely rewarding experience.

The sources of these activities are numerous. I designed many of them as the need arose in the training seminars that I conduct each week. Others are modified from existing games and activities I have learned from others in the field. I apologize in advance to anyone I may not have given credit to for their activity.

Thank you Lynn Ellis and Marta Frey for giving me the opportunity to develop training classes and activities at the Collin County SBDC.

My thanks to the many talented and gifted speakers and trainers in my life who are always there with encouragement and words of wisdom. Thanks to the Charleston Group who in 2008 challenged me to launch to the next level. It's been a wild ride!

Special thanks to Jonathan Peters, the ultimate wordsmith, for always giving me the better way to phrase things.

Finally, thank you to my sons Lou, Nick and Joe for listening with enthusiasm and giving feedback as I experiment with new activities and ideas ... I love you guys!

INTRODUCTION

Imagine your workshops alive with activity, interaction, and excitement within the opening minutes. When you use the activities in this book you will feel the change in atmosphere from the traditional lecture seminar, to one where participants are involved in the learning process right from the start.

As a trainer, it is up to you to create this environment in your training room. There are strategic steps that you can do to accomplish this:

- Involve participants in an activity in the first five minutes
- Frequently check for understanding
- Modify plans based on participant feedback
- Use self-disclosure and humor to develop an open climate
- Use a wide variety of learning methods
- Give the what, why, and how for every training activity

The activities in this book are quick and to the point. Each activity lets you know what materials you need, what to say to set up the activity, and how to handle the all important debrief at the end of each activity.

You will notice that many of the activities instruct you to:

> Divide your class into small groups. Instruct
> them that they should move into teams of no
> less than 4 and no more than 6.

Studies show that adults will learn best when they have an opportunity to interact with their peers.

The arguments for using active learning in the classroom are clear. Moving around a room, participating in a contest, or simply talking to other students can raise the level of activity to a point where a participant is more alert and attentive to the content of the class. Using activities in a training session encourages active learning, as well as collaboration and interactivity.

Some activities in this book suggest awarding prizes for the team winners. Any small token will do -- chocolate, pens, Post-It Notes™, binder clips. The item is not as important as acknowledging the team's accomplishment with praise. The real point is that participation in the activity requires the learner to use the content presented and work with the ideas taught.

Throughout the book you will see special tips called the Fantastic Five. These are fundamentals that you can easily follow and use in your training environments. The fundamentals will teach you how to establish clear objectives and goals, define the purpose, present instructions and evaluate the results of the activities that you select for your training sessions.

Help yourself by using these ready-made activities. When you bring these activities into your training room, you are providing rich educational experiences and learning that transfers beyond the classroom. *As a result, your excellent training will act as the gateway to your organization's other services.*

Plus—to help keep you on the cutting edge of training and development tools, we've added a **NEW** section on Gamification to show you how to use Gamification in your organization! See *Game On!* starting on p. 122.

All the activities in this guide book can be used in a gamified training. As you will learn, Gamification does NOT mean that you have to be a gamer or a techie, OR that you need expensive software.

You owe it to yourself and your clients to give these Totally Awesome Training Activities a try!

Section 1

Nuts and Bolts

Nuts and Bolts

1. **Who are your participants - and how can you establish rapport with them?**
   - ►Who will be attending?
   - ►How will you make your content relevant for that demographic?
   - ►What is your objective for the training?

2. **What is the best way to arrange the room set-up?**
   - ►Participants should be able to easily see you and each other. Nothing kills interaction faster than when participants cannot see and hear each other.
   - ►Repeat questions and remarks made by individuals so that everyone in the room can hear them.

3. **When do you start to build credibility?**
   - ►Your credibility as a leader depends on your ability to get the group's attention quickly.
   - ►Adults learn from someone they respect and like.
   - ►You can be fun and funny - without being silly.
   - ►Know your material well, so you can confidently move away from your notes.

4. **Where do you begin? Begin with a bang!**
   ▶ If your participants had to leave after the first 15 minutes of training, would they feel like they got their money's worth?
   ▶ Memorize your first few sentences so you can put yourself on auto-pilot.
   ▶ Practice smiling in front of a mirror so your face knows what a smile feels like.

5. **Ask yourself, why are you using audiovisual equipment?**
   ▶ Will it actually help or hurt your training?
   ▶ When you use visual aids, the group's focus is divided. How can you keep the focus on you and keep distractions to a minimum?
   ▶ Avoid monotonous slide after slide presentations and repeatedly "flying in" bullet points at every chance you get.
   ▶ Strategically use effects to emphasize your points. Don't just point out your knowledge of effects.

If You Build It ...
(And other Business Myths)

Purpose: To illustrate to your participants that most people have mistaken perceptions about their products and services.

Materials: None

How to: Ask the group to define "myth." Allow the group to give you some definitions, and then you can summarize that a *myth is a widely held but mistaken belief.* To help illustrate the definition give some of the following examples:

- The check is in the mail.
- Lose weight while you sleep.
- It will only take a minute to fix this.
- One size fits all.
- Everybody is doing it.
- You're only as old as you feel.

Then add one or more myths that are relevant to your training topic, such as:
- There are government grants to start your small business.
- Once our customers see our product it will sell itself.
- As soon as my website is up I'll have more customers than I know what to do with.
- We won't be able to keep these products on the shelf.
- Our process will be much easier, faster, cheaper, better, etc.

Debrief
Questions: ▶ Where do these myths come from?
                 ▶ Are they indeed a myth, or is there truth in them?
                 ▶ What can you do to turn the myth into reality?

Awesome
Tip: Be aware that most of your class fully believes these business myths. You will have to tread carefully in these waters. If you have some seasoned business owners in your class, you can ask them for examples of myths that they once believed and how they have changed their outlook and strategy.

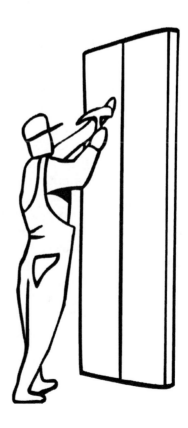

Pieces of Me

Purpose: To help participants get to know each other by building a puzzle about themselves.

Materials: White board, flip chart, or projector and screen.

How to: Divide your class into small groups. Instruct them that they should move into teams of no less than 4 and no more than 6.

You can project a picture of <u>six</u> puzzle pieces onto your screen or use a flip chart paper that has puzzle pieces drawn on it. Each of the puzzle pieces contains a question that the participants should answer.

> *Example:*
> Current occupation?
> Family, spouse, children?
> Pets? Hobbies?
> Favorite movie or line from a movie?
> If "your song" played when you entered the
>   room, what would that song be?
> Little known fact?
> Greatest risk ever taken?

You can also include topic specific questions in the last 2 puzzle pieces – such as –
>   What is your greatest concern about starting
>   a business?
>   Why is now a good time to start this business?

Give each participant just 1-2 minutes to walk through the entire puzzle and answer the questions.

Ask one person in the group to start and then work clockwise through the group so that everyone gets a chance to share with their group mates something about themselves.

Debrief
Questions: ▶ What did you learn about each other?
▶ How difficult or easy was it to share information about yourself with others?
▶ Is it important to know the people you are working with?
▶ Why?

Awesome
Tips: The idea is to start with the easy questions to get the participants comfortable with the activity. As they move through the puzzle pieces, the questions become more in depth.

♪kittle ♪kattle

Purpose: To get your group immediately involved with each other, and to begin to develop a team dynamic.

Materials: Large bag of Skittles®, M&M's®, or other candy.

How to: Divide your class into small groups. Instruct them that they should move into teams of no less than 4 and no more than 6.

Have each participant take a couple pieces of candy. Be sure to tell them, "Don't eat them yet!" Going clockwise around the circle, use a color-coded set of questions that they will share with their team members.

Example:

Blue	time you felt very proud
Green	leader you respect and why
Yellow	time you were scared
Orange	time when you failed
Red	time you felt embarrassed

Debrief Questions:
► Why is it important for us to learn about people in our network?
► How difficult (or easy) was it to share information about yourself with others?
► How can we learn more about other small business owners such as ourselves?

Awesome
Tips: Be sure to project the color-coded questions onto the screen, or display the code on a flip chart or white board. This way your participants can refer back to the code during the activity.

Feel free to change the color codes and questions to fit your training content.

What's in a N.A.M.E.

Purpose: To loosen people up and start building a team dynamic. This exercise is a fun, non-threatening way for people to get to know each other.

Materials: Paper and writing utensils.

How to: Divide your class into small groups. Instruct them that they should move into teams of no less than 4 and no more than 6.

Ask the group to write their name on a piece of paper. Tell them that they should now view their names as an acronym – each letter stands for something about them.

Example:
Lindsey – L is for love chocolate. I is for I'm an Indie music fan. N is for Nashville, where I'm from. S is for sounds, because I like all different kinds of sounds. E is for egg drop soup, my favorite, and Y is for you, because I want to know more about you.

Give them 5 minutes to think of interesting facts about themselves that correspond with the letters of their first name. Then have each participant share their acronym with their group.

Debrief Questions:
- ► What did you learn about each other?
- ► How difficult or easy was it to share information about yourself with others?
- ► **What interesting things did you learn about your team mates?**

► Is it important to know the people you are working with? Why?

Awesome Tips: You can also use this activity in a group of people who are already familiar with each other. It is a great way to learn little-known facts, hobbies, interests, and build a deeper understanding of who the individuals are.

10 Things in Common

Purpose: To help people see that they have more things in common with others than they may have initially thought.

Materials: None

How to: Divide your class into small groups. Instruct them that they should move into teams of no less than 4 and no more than 6.

Explain some concepts of team dynamics and high performing teams. For example, high performing teams have a purpose. They are empowered to act. Each member is responsible for their own actions.

Remind them that when we form new teams, there is always the initial phase of getting to know each other. Ask them, "Have you ever looked at the team and thought, 'I have nothing in common with anyone else on the team'?" Then state, "Well, I'm going to help you see just how much in common you actually have."

Tell the groups that they have 3 minutes to come up with a list of 10 things that they have in common with the rest of the members of their group. All members of the group must be in agreement that it is a common element among all of them for it to count on their list.

As they start to come up with their 10 things in common, interrupt them and say, "Oh, by the way, did I mention that you cannot use work related items, such as 'We are all small business owners.'?"

Pause to let them groan for a moment, and then add, "Also, you may not use any body parts or articles of clothing, such as 'We all have two eyes', or 'We're all wearing shoes.' OK, now find 10 things you all have in common."

Let them know when there is 1 minute left. When time has expired, have them share their team list with the rest of the room. This creates a wonderful opportunity for camaraderie, laughter, and relationship building.

Debrief Questions:
- ▶ How hard or easy was it for you to find 10 things in common?
- ▶ Were you able to find 10 things in 3 minutes?
- ▶ Did you discover that you have more things in common than you thought you did?
- ▶ How can this help you in the marketplace?

Awesome Tips:

The very act of setting a time limit and making it somewhat of a competition immediately begins to build a team dynamic. Observe how the teams start to work together, and/or how dominant personalities start to take-charge in order to accomplish the task and "win the competition." You can point out what you observed during your debrief questions, but be careful not to pass judgment or point the finger at any individual.

Trash or Treasure

Purpose: To find significance and selling points in objects that may seem to not have any value.

Materials: Various assorted objects. Go to a dollar or discount store, or even a flea market, and pick up unusual items to use as sample products.

How to: Divide your class into small groups. Instruct them that they should move into teams of no less than 4 and no more than 6.

Have the participants identify their market niche for the object, and even develop a market and pricing strategy. Give them 5 minutes to do this and then have them share with the group.

Debrief Questions:
- ▶ Was this exercise easy or difficult? Why?
- ▶ How creative do you think you were?
- ▶ Did you work under any assumptions that you now think limited your creativity?
- ▶ How can this help you in the marketplace?

Awesome Tips: Be sure to include a wide variety of objects that will require creative thinking. Don't be afraid to have fun with it. *If you pick interesting and fun objects, your participants will be interested and have fun as well.*

Notes

Heroes take journeys, confront dragons,
and discover the treasure of their true selves.
- Carol Lynn Pearson

Cash Bonus

Purpose: To give everyone a chance to learn one interesting fact about the other members of their team. Participants will begin to connect on a personal level, and as a result, feel more comfortable sharing thoughts and questions as the class progresses.

Materials: Assortment of coins. You can use all of one denomination or a combination of pennies, nickels, dimes and quarters.

How to: Divide your class into small groups. Instruct them that they should move into teams of no less than 4 and no more than 6.

Pass out one coin to each participant. *As you pass out the coins you can joke with the participants by asking them if they realized they were going to receive a "cash bonus" for attending the class.*

Ask them to first introduce themselves with their names and any other information you want them to share. Then ask them to share something significant or interesting about themselves from the year on the coin. You can go first to give them an example.

For example: "Hi, my name is Monica. I'm a serial entrepreneur. I've had some businesses that I've been able to grow and sell, and I've had others that were great learning experiences! My coin says 1988. That happens to be the year my son Joe was born. He was my third boy, but I thought I was going to have a girl. I had even decorated the nursery in pink."

Debrief

Questions: ▶ How difficult or easy was it for you to think of something that happened in the year on the coin?
▶ Did you mind sharing that information with the people in your group?
▶ If so, why was it difficult?
▶ What is the application for this information back in the marketplace?

Awesome
Tips: Make sure the coins are dated within the past 20 years. If someone is having a difficult time remembering something from their specific year, encourage them to describe what was going on in their life at that time, such as, what job they had, were they still in school, etc.

e of Success

Purpose: To demonstrate how beliefs and values may change with age, maturity, and experience.

Materials: None

How to: Divide your class into small groups. Instruct them that they should move into teams of no less than 4 and no more than 6.

Ask them to individually write out the answers to the following questions:

"When you were in elementary school, how did you define success?"

"When you were in your early 20's, how did you define success?"

"Right now – how do you define success?"

After each participant has written their answers, ask them to share their pictures of success with their team members. Allot 5 minutes for them to discuss their answers. When time has expired ask the entire group to share some of the interesting pictures of success that were shared.

Debrief Questions:
► How many of you identified success when you were a child as: being a ballerina, fireman, making a $1,000,000, or becoming a movie star?
► Did those answers change when you were in your 20's?

21

▶ Are the answers the same or different now? Why does our picture of success change?

Awesome
Tips: While this should be a fun and light-hearted activity, it is also important to tie it back to a picture of success for their business. *Many small business owners get their business started without a picture of what a successful business looks like.* Help them to understand that there is no right or wrong answer to what success looks like, but that it is important to develop a picture of success.

Lions, Tigers, and Bears

Purpose: To demonstrate that everyone has obstacles in their life that must be overcome.

Materials: White Board or Flip Chart and Markers

How to: Describe a scene of walking in a forest. Give details about the time of day, weather, and your general state of mind. Reveal that you have rounded a corner and come face-to-face with a grizzly bear. (If you prefer, you can make your story about an African Safari and use a lion or tiger.)

Ask your participants to give one-word responses as to what they would do in that situation. Record their answers on a flip chart or white board.

Then say to your participants, "The answers that you just gave reveals how you respond to the 'bears' you meet everyday. The bears represent the problems you face daily in your business."

Debrief Questions:
► What kind of "bears" do you face in your business?
► How do you typically respond to those "bears"?
► Is there a response that would be more productive?
► How can you plan for those "bears" in the future?

**Awesome
Tip:**   This is an opportunity to share how your
organization can help them with solutions when
they face the *"bears"* in their business. Encourage
them to stay plugged in and to use you as a
resource for *"bear hunting"*.

Section 2

Position Your Point

Position Your Point

1. **Use an engaging game or activity that strategically sets up the seminar.** Pick any number of exercises from this activity book to accomplish this.

2. **Use real-life or fictional stories.** You can choose a funny story, a dramatic anecdote, or an example involving emotional pain to grab your audiences' attention.

3. **Show a dramatic or humorous video that visually communicates the main points of the training.** As you come across fun, interesting, or motivating videos, save them in a file on your computer so that you can easily reference them for your different training topics.

4. **Offer a relevant case study that applies an element of realism.** Help the audience identify their attitude about the topic and then work together to apply problem-solving skills.

5. **Give them a short quiz.** The questions are relevant to your topic. *Make the quiz fun by reviewing answers in a game show atmosphere.* Reward them for correct responses with a

simple "good answer" or tossing pieces of candy. Remind them there is no grade, and an incorrect response requires nothing more than a good-natured smile and buzzer sound effect. *Stay light-hearted and have fun. If you laugh, so will they.*

Shoe Salesman

Purpose: To encourage creative thinking in selling what may seem to be a difficult product to sell.

Materials: Prizes

How to: Divide your class into small groups. Instruct them that they should move into teams of no less than 4 and no more than 6.

Tell them the following story: The Old Woman who lives in a shoe is moving. The shoe is pretty worn out (and smelly), after years of housing the old woman and all of her children. The Old Woman has asked your team to help sell the shoe. You have 8 minutes to determine what other nursery rhyme character might want to buy the shoe and to create a sales pitch aimed directly at them. When your planning time expires, you will have 2 minutes to try to sell the shoe. You'll receive a prize if you can actually sell your shoe and if all members of your team participate in the presentation.

Give them time to work in their team to generate ideas. Be sure to let them know when there are 5 minutes and 3 minutes left on the clock so they have time to create their sales presentation.

Debrief Questions:
- ►How many of you thought this exercise was silly?
- ►Was it easy or hard to sell the shoe? Why?
- ►How can this help you in the marketplace?

Awesome
Tips: Encourage your participants to get as creative as they would like, since it is only an exercise. However, in real-world situations, this type of creative thinking can be extremely useful in marketing your products or services.

Dirty Laundry

Purpose: Use as an in-house training exercise to warm up your team for more challenging exercises.

Materials: None

How to: Begin with a zany exercise in which the team brainstorms as many uses for dirty t-shirts as they can think of. How would they market the t-shirts to the public? Ask the team to select their two most original ideas.

Next, ask your team to generate new ways to market your organization's services. As ideas surface, only allow questions to clarify contributions. *Do not cheer or boo any suggestions.*

The team will eagerly discuss the ideas they believe are worthy of pursuing and it will be tough to select the best ideas.

Debrief Questions:
- ▶ Was it easy or hard to sell the dirty t-shirts? Why?
- ▶ How creative do you think you were?
- ▶ Did you work under any assumptions that you now think limited your creativity?
- ▶ How can this help you in the marketplace?

Awesome Tips: Encourage your participants to get as creative as they would like, since it is only an exercise. However, in real-world situations, this type of creative thinking can be extremely useful in marketing your products or services.

Notes

In the factory we make cosmetics, in the drugstore we sell hope.
- Charles Revson

Window Screens

Purpose: To improve thinking and selling skills. Participants can practice creative marketing ideas and learn how to look at things from a different perspective.

Materials: Prizes

How to: Divide your class into small groups. Instruct them that they should move into teams of no less than 4 and no more than 6.

Read the following lead-in to the group:

"Your company has just been given a truck load of old window screens. Instead of paying to haul them off to the dump, your team has been given the assignment to think of a product that can be made with these screens. Your team will receive a bonus if it can sell the screens and make a profit.

You have 8 minutes to generate your ideas and select the one idea which you believe will be the most profitable. After you have selected the best idea, your team should prepare a 60-second commercial for marketing your new product."

Give them time to work in their team to generate ideas. Be sure to let them know when there are 5 minutes and 3 minutes left on the clock so they have time to create their commercial.

Each team should then present their commercial to the rest of the group. Have the entire group vote on which idea is likely to be the most profitable.

Note: If the group is highly competitive, make it a rule that participants cannot vote for their team's idea.

**Debrief
Questions:** ▶How creative do you think you were?
▶Did you work under any assumptions that you now think limited your creativity?
▶How did your team arrive at the best idea to market?
▶How can this help you in the marketplace?

**Awesome
Tips:** You may want to come up with some product ideas yourself before the exercise begins such as: cutting the screens into a variety of circles to use in the bottom of potted plants so the water drains from the roots. Or, you could make a bug cage to capture fire flies. If a team is really stuck, offer your ideas to get their creativity flowing.

Here's Your Sign

Purpose: To emphasize clarity in marketing.

Materials: White board, flip chart, or projector and screen.

How to: Divide your class into small groups. Instruct them that they should move into teams of no less than 4 and no more than 6.

Read the following lead-in to the group:

"Driving down the road you see countless billboards. Open a magazine and you flip through page after page of advertisements. Click to a website and view information and banner ads. Read a newspaper and mixed with the news are print ads for all types of products and services. All of these are designed to get you to do something or buy something.

But have you ever seen an advertisement that left you scratching your head in wonder? Here is a chance to come up with some clever explanations of your own. In this exercise you'll be shown ads with unclear meanings. It is your job to come up with as many potential answers as possible."

For example — Wanted CFD — could mean ... Wanted: Clean, fun, drummer.

Below are numerous combinations of mystery ads:
- Stop at the Pear Tree Inn for some KPT.
- Visit LMP for the thrill of a lifetime!
- Save the world from MPR.

- Get your SVN now!
- Join the PLU Saturday night!
- RWP -- Where all your dreams come true!
- Get your TDB now!

Project the ads onto a screen or write them on a whiteboard or flip chart. Record the groups' responses on the white board or flip chart as the ideas are generated. If you have divided the group into smaller teams, assign each team a different ad and ask them to record their answers individually. You can then have each team report their responses to the entire group.

Debrief Questions:

▶ Have you ever seen an acronym you didn't understand?

▶ Have you ever used an acronym that other people may have not understood?

▶ What elements in your marketing my be unclear?

▶ How can this help you in the marketplace?

Awesome Tips:

The three letters included in each of the ads are random. Stretch their creativity by repeating the phrase and changing the three letters.

Begin at the End

Purpose: To encourage creative thinking and analytical thought progressions.

Materials: White board, flip chart, or projector and screen.

How to: Divide your class into small groups. Instruct them that they should move into teams of no less than 4 and no more than 6.

Read the following lead-in to the group:

"Questions are usually followed by answers. In this exercise we have turned it around. You will be given the answer first, and your assignment as a team is to come up with a list of questions that could possibly contribute to that answer.

For example, the answer is red. What is the question?
    What color is an apple?
    What is my favorite color?
    What is a newspaper?
    What color are my cheeks when I blush?
    What is the NY Times Best Sellers list?"

Then tell them that they have 2 minutes to come up with as many questions as possible for the following answers. Only give them one answer at a time. You do not have to use all the answers listed, but start with the easy ones like peanut butter and ice cream, and work your way towards more abstract concepts.

- The answer is peanut butter. What is the question?
- The answer is ice cream. What is the question?
- The answer is cooperation. What is the question?
- The answer is location, location, location. What is the question?
- The answer is imagination. What is the question?
- The answer is hopeless. What is the question?
- The answer is common sense. What is the question?

Debrief Questions:
▶ How creative do you think you were?
▶ Did you work under any assumptions that you now think limited your creativity?
▶ Were you surprised with some of your team member's questions?
▶ How can this help you in the marketplace?

Awesome Tips:

> By stating the answer first, participants must rearrange their thought processes and work back to what the beginning might have been. This *backward progression* helps participants to realize that their employees and customers must also make similar assumptions.

Write the answers on a white board or flip chart. If you divide the participants into small groups, ask each team to elect one member to act as a scribe for their group to record answers.

You can choose to either assign the same answers to all teams or divide the answers among the teams so that they are all making different backward progressions.

A.B.C.?

Purpose: To help your participants think creatively and respond quickly. You can use it to lead into training on product development, marketing, finding a niche, meeting a need with your product, etc.

Materials: Prizes

How to: Divide your class into small groups. Instruct them that they should move into teams of no less than 4 and no more than 6.

Read the following lead-in to the group:

"The U.S. Secretary of Education has decided that adding a twenty-seventh letter to the alphabet will improve literacy. Your assignment as a team is to invent the letter that will be the most beneficial. You have 5 minutes to decide upon the sound and the symbol for your new letter. Your team will then have 1 minute to present your new letter to the Secretary of Education. If your letter is chosen, you will get the opportunity and honor to attend a black tie dinner at the White House to receive recognition for your contribution."

Each team should then present their new letter to the rest of the group. Have the entire group vote on which idea is likely to be the most feasible. Note: If the team is highly competitive, make it a rule that participants cannot vote for their team's idea.

Debrief

Questions: ▶ How creative do you think you were?

▶ Did you work under any assumptions that you now think limited your creativity?

▶ How did your team arrive at the best idea to market?

▶ How can this help you in the marketplace?

Awesome

Tips: The time is limited so that your group is required to think fast, and maybe even get a little silly. *Laughter and creativity have a direct correlation to each other, so encourage your group to go ahead and have fun with both the exercise and their presentation.*

Gotta Get a Gimmick

Purpose: To show your participants the importance of identifying what makes their product or service uniquely different.

Materials: Shop at your local grocer and pick up some of the following items: Pillsbury crescent rolls or cookie dough tube, Oscar Meyer wieners, Frosted Flakes cereal and Snuggle fabric softener.

Also, pick up some items that do not have an identifiable gimmick. Be creative. Choose both food and non-food items.

How to: Bring the materials to class with you and set up the exercise as follows:

Divide your class into small groups. Instruct them that they should move into teams of no less than 4 and no more than 6.

After they are in their small groups, give each of the teams one of the items that you purchased at the store that does not have an identifiable gimmick.

Then say to the class as you hold up the items: "Pillsbury has the Dough Boy, Snuggles Fabric Softener has Snuggles the Bear, Oscar Meyer has the Weiner Mobile, and Frosted Flakes has Tony the Tiger. Your assignment is to create an original gimmick for your team's product. You have 8 minutes to create the gimmick and then 1 minute to present your gimmick to the rest of the group in the form of a commercial. Your commercial should include customer testimonials about your product and refer to the gimmick."

Give them time to work in their team to generate ideas. Be sure to let them know when there are 5-minutes and 3-minutes left on the clock, so they have time to create their commercial.

Each team should then present their commercial to the rest of the group. Have the entire group vote on which gimmick is likely to be the most marketable. Note: If the team is highly competitive, make it a rule that participants cannot vote for their team's idea.

Debrief
Questions:
▶ How creative do you think you were?
▶ Did you work under any assumptions that you now think limited your creativity?
▶ How did your team arrive at the best gimmick idea?
▶ How can this help you in the marketplace?

Awesome
Tips:
A great lead-in to this exercise is to use an excerpt from the movie *Gypsy*, a 1962 musical made by Warner Bros. starring Natalie Woods. In one scene, Natalie's character is about to join the burlesque troop, and the other dancers warn her that to be a success, she's *"Gotta Get a Gimmick."* It's a fun, harmless number that will get your participants involved, laughing, and even singing along!

Contributed by Elyse Eriksson

Tooty Fruity Juice

Purpose: To help your participants think creatively and respond quickly. You can use it to lead into training on product development, marketing, finding a niche market, meeting a need with your product, etc.

Materials: Prizes

How to: Divide your class into small groups. Instruct them that they should move into teams of no less than 4 and no more than 6.

Read the following lead-in to the group.

"After much experimentation, a chemist has developed a no-fruit juice called, *Tooty Fruity Juice*. Made entirely in a laboratory, the juice will replace the need for fruit orchards. Better yet, the chemist claims that the juice will improve memory, help people to lose weight, and even increase psychic abilities in some consumers. Critics of the juice are concerned about the future of the fruit farmer.

Your team will unveil the new juice at an upcoming food convention. You have 8 minutes to plan a presentation selling the attendees on the benefits of this new product. Your presentation must include a slogan for *Tooty Fruity Juice* and a jingle. When planning time expires, you will have 2 minutes to make your presentation."

Give them time to work in their team to generate ideas. Be sure to let them know when there are

5 minutes and 3 minutes left on the clock, so they have time to create their presentation.

Each team should then present to the rest of the group. Have the entire group vote on which idea is likely to be the most profitable. Note: If the team is highly competitive, make it a rule that participants cannot vote for their team's idea.

Debrief Questions:
▶ How creative do you think you were?
▶ Did you work under any assumptions that you now think limited your creativity?
▶ How did your team arrive at the slogan and jingle?
▶ How can this help you in the marketplace?

Awesome Tips:
To increase buy-in and participation from your group, you can bring in "samples" of the *Tooty Fruity Juice*. Use a fruit-flavored, sugar-free drink for your sample, or a product like Sunny Delight.

Draw a Parallel

Purpose: To help make a connection between two seemingly unrelated things.

Materials: White board, flip chart, or projector and screen.

How to: Divide your class into small groups. Instruct them that they should move into teams of no less than 4 and no more than 6.

Read the following lead-in to the group:

"Given two seemingly unrelated items, can you make a connection between them? For example, a number of possibilities arise when asked to make a connection between a tent and a car:

You can pack your tent in your car.
You can sleep in a tent or you can sleep in your car.
A tent and a car both use metal parts.
You can run from a bear and try to hide in both a tent or a car.

Your team has 2-minutes to come up with as many connections as possible between the following items:"

Note: Only give them one set of seemingly unrelated words at a time.

- Make a connection between a straw and a chicken.
- Make a connection between a pen and a computer.
- Make a connection between a light bulb and a camera.

45

- Make a connection between a book and a bicycle.
- Make a connection between a sock and a noodle.
- Make a connection between a paperclip and a screwdriver.
- Make a connection between a lamp and a flower.
- Make a connection between an ant and an apple.
- Make a connection between a carrot and a mouse.

Debrief
Questions: ► What did you learn?
► What insights did you have during the activity?
► How creative do you think you were?
► How can this help you in the marketplace?

Awesome
Tips: Motivational Speaker Keith Craft has a saying, "The thing is never about the thing, but everything is about everything." In marketing they will have to help their customers make the connection between the product and service they are offering, and the need or want of the customer.

Write the unrelated words on a white board or flip chart, or project them onto a screen. If you divide the participants into small groups, ask each team to elect one member to act as a scribe for their group to record answers.

Choose to either assign the same set of words to all teams or divide the sets among the teams so that they are all making different connections. You may choose to do a couple connections with the entire group as a warm up, and then have the individual teams work on their own connections.

Confrontation is not a 4-Letter Word

Purpose: To role-play an activity that gives participants practice in handling conflict and confrontation.

Materials: None

How to: First teach your participants the 5-Step Strategy for Confrontation:
1. **Paint the Big Picture** – state to the person: "Here's what I observe – sometimes …"
2. **"For example …"**
   Specific date, time, place
   Behavior – not personality
   Observed by me
3. **"Here's what would be more productive …"**
4. **"When you do this …"**
   Here's the benefit you're going to get
5. **"Can I count on you to …"**
   Always a question
   Wait for answer
   Follow up

Next, ask the participants to write down the initials of a person that they have conflict with.

Then ask them to partner up with someone else in the class. After each person has found a partner, ask one person in the pair to be Partner A and the other person to be Partner B – they can choose which is which.

Ask Partner A to tell their partner who the person is in their life that they are having conflict with and what type of conflict it is. Tell the participants that it is OK to change names to protect the innocent if they are uncomfortable with revealing too much information. It is Partner B's job to temporarily become that person.

Partner A should now walk through the 5-steps listed above and "practice" confronting with their partner. Give them about 5 minutes to do this and then have them switch – so that each gets the opportunity to "practice" confrontation.

Debrief
Questions:
▶ How did it feel to confront?
▶ Did the person listen or give you arguments?
▶ What other skills would be helpful for you in handling confrontation?
▶ How can this help you in the marketplace?

Awesome
Tip:
Be sure to use the words "practice" or "lab." If you tell people they are going to role-play confrontation skills – they will be resistant to the idea and perhaps feel self-conscious or irritated about participating in such an exercise.

When you tell them they get to practice in a safe environment, they are very receptive to it. They can then use the skill in dealing with vendors, customers, employees – just about anyone in their life.

Back to the Future

Purpose: To demonstrate how easy it is to see where we've been, and how difficult it can be to plan where we are going.

Materials: None

How to: Ask your participants to get on their feet and partner with someone who they have not yet met. Then tell them "We're going back in time – back to the good 'ole days. Imagine that it is 10 years ago. For some of you, you were kids, for others it seems like just yesterday." Ask the participants, "What were you doing back then? Were you still in school? What job did you have? Were you married? Did you have children? Or had you even reached puberty yet?"

Now have them introduce themselves to their partner as if it were 10 years ago. People enjoy this because it gives them a chance to laugh and reminisce.

After a few minutes ask them to stop and tell them, "Now we're going to the future. I want you to imagine that it is 10 years from now. Where will you be? What will you be doing? Is your business going strong, or are you retired on a beach somewhere? How do you see your future?"

This one is a little tougher, but some people will dive right in with how they see their future. You can use good debrief questions to lead them into teaching on planning, empowerment, living with a purpose, legacy, and many other directions.

Debrief
Questions: ►How did it feel to look back?
►Were those the good ole' days?
►How did it feel to look towards the future?
►Will it require some planning?
►What actions steps can you execute to create that future?

Awesome
Tips: While this should be a fun and lighthearted activity, it is important to emphasize that to get where we envision ourselves in the future, it takes some planning.

Power Negotiating

Purpose: To help participants find creative solutions to simple problems; they see that a majority vote is not always the most effective way to decide.

Materials: Two quarters for each team.

How to: Divide the group into teams of three. Give each team two quarters. They have three minutes to decide between the three of them who will keep the coins. If all else fails, a majority vote can decide. After three minutes, any team still undecided will lose the coins back to you.

Debrief Questions:
► What strategies did you use during the negotiation?
► Which were most helpful?
► Did everyone rely on majority rules? Why or Why not?
► Did the time limit effect the decision?
► Did you find out anything about your group?
► How can this help you in the marketplace?

Awesome Tips: Be sure to emphasize that whoever ends up with the coins gets to keep them.

Notes

Let us never negotiate out of fear.
But let us never fear to negotiate.
- John Fitzgerald Kennedy

So What?

Purpose: To help your participants translate the features of their products and services into benefit language.

Materials: Paper and writing utensils.

How to: Divide your class into small groups. Instruct them that they should move into teams of no less than 4 and no more than 6.

Ask them to write on a piece of paper at least 3 qualities or features about their products or services. Give them a few minutes to write these out.

After they have written the features, tell them to read the features to their team members. Their team members are to respond with "So What?" By answering that question, your participants should drill down to what is the real benefit of their product for the customer. Go around the team clockwise with each person taking turns reading their product features.

If your participants need some help getting started you can use this example: "Suppose I sell printers, and I tell you that a feature of my printer is that it prints with 1200 dpi quality. Your response would be "So What?" In reality you may not even know what 1200 dpi quality means. However if I tell you that with this printer you can create professional-looking documents and the ability to produce marketing materials in-house instead of going to the local print shop — are you now interested in my printer?"

Debrief

Questions: ▶ Were you able to come up with features for you products or service?

▶ How difficult was it to translate the features into benefits?

▶ How can this help you in the marketplace?

Awesome

Tip: This exercise is tough. Encourage the teams to help their members create benefit language when they get stuck. The synergy of the team will produce some awesome benefits that the members can use in the marketplace.

Tell Me No

Purpose: To get your participants talking about their products and services and hear the possible objections that they may get from potential customers or clients.

Materials: None

How to: Divide your class into small groups. Instruct them that they should move into teams of no less than 4 and no more than 6.

Read the following lead-in to the group:

"Traditionally, market research can cost you thousands of dollars. We're going to do some market research right here in class that, if you are open to it, will prove to be priceless to you and your business.

Your assignment is to share your business idea with the members of your team. Your team's job is to listen to your ideas and raise any questions or concerns they have about your concept. Your job at that point is to not get offended or defensive, but rather to listen to their questions and concerns and evaluate how you can overcome their objections.

Team members – it will be far more beneficial for your teammates if you raise your questions and concerns about their business idea – rather than tell them what a great idea they have. Lots of people will tell them that. It is your job to help them get better."

Be sure to allot enough time for everyone to share their idea and receive feedback. You should plan 3-5 minutes for each person in the small groups. Keep a careful watch on the time, and be sure to let the group know how much time is remaining.

Debrief Questions:
▶ How did it feel when people raised objections to your ideas?
▶ Did you feel like they were telling you that your baby is ugly?
▶ Did you get defensive or listen to their ideas?
▶ What did you learn?
▶ Will this be valuable to you?
▶ How can this help you in the marketplace?

Awesome Tips:

> Often times your participants get married to their logo, business name, product delivery technique, and any other number of items in their business. This activity, in a safe environment, gives them the opportunity to do some free "market research".

If your class does this exercise in the right spirit, and really works on giving feedback instead of kudos, it will prove to be the most valuable and well-liked activity that you do in training.

Your participants will be having so much fun, and learning so much about their business and others, that it is difficult to pull them back into the training. Plan ahead so that you can graciously give them another 5 minutes, and not be behind in your class schedule.

Brag Fest

Purpose: To help participants discover and reveal resources that already exist inside of them in a quiet and intense way.

Materials: Paper and pens/markers.

How to: Divide your class into small groups. Instruct them that they should move into teams of no less than 4 and no more than 6. Give everyone paper and pens.

Have each person draw a picture of the achievement of which they feel most proud. Matchstick figures are perfectly acceptable. The achievement can be from any time in their lives. It may be from home, work, social, academic, or a hobby. It can be a particular instant or something that took a period of time. After a few minutes, have them write on the borders of their pictures all the personal qualities they needed to bring about that achievement.

Give them 5 minutes to work on drawing their achievements. When they have finished, ask them to discuss their individual achievements and qualities with the people in their group.

Debrief Questions:
- ▶ Did you find it difficult to "*brag*" about your achievements?
- ▶ What other resources should you be tapping into?
- ▶ Given these qualities, what, are you capable of achieving?

Awesome

Tips: Ask the participants to not be modest when defining their qualities. It is easy to feel boastful, but those are all real life characteristics that we need to identify to help achieve difficult goals.

Also, take this opportunity to educate them about the resources that your organization has to help them.

Juice or Jam?

Purpose: To improve conflict management and negotiation skills.

Materials: Bag of oranges. Directions for Groups A and B on slips of paper.

How to: Ask the participants to sit in groups of three and choose to be either A, B, or C. Give each group an orange.

Bring the A's together and pass a slip of paper around to them that says, "You must not reveal that you need all the orange peel to make marmalade."

Now bring the B's together. Pass a slip of paper around to them that says, "You must not reveal that you need all the orange innards to make a drink."

Tell the class, "A and B each want the orange, and it is C's task to find a solution to this conflict that both A and B will be happy with. A and B can argue why they deserve the orange but neither can reveal their secret."

This should lead to C trying to divide the orange in different ways, but not thinking of dividing it into peel and innards. After five minutes, reveal A's and B's secrets, and share ideas with the class.

Debrief Questions:
- ►How many ways might the orange be divided?
- ►Could the conflict have been resolved more easily if people had known each other's motives?
- ►How can this help you in the marketplace?

Awesome

Tips: Allow the teams to keep the oranges to eat if they'd like. Be sure to have napkins and a trash can.

Section 3

Connect and Engage

Connect and Engage

1. **Use examples as much as possible.** Provide real-life illustrations of the points you are making. Use anonymous examples from other clients, or use your own successes and/ or failures as relevant examples of what and what not to do when starting or running a business.

2. **Guided note taking.** Provide instructions or a form indicating how participants should take notes during the training. For example, in a customer service class, ask them to draw a T-chart with one column representing good customer service and the other representing bad customer service. Participants can then recall their own experiences and fill in accordingly.

3. **Illuminators.** These are brief, quick, activities that illuminate the information, ideas, and skills you are presenting.

4. **Visual Backups.** Think about how you can put presentation tools in your participants hands that help them see as well as hear what you are saying.

5. **Movement.** If nothing else it will help keep your participants awake. Make it your goal to get them up out of their seat, if only for a minute or two, at least once every 45 minutes.

Gutter Clutter

Purpose: To provide a fun and creative way to help participants evaluate beliefs and behaviors that help or hinder their business.

Materials: Flip chart paper and markers for each team.

How to: Divide your class into small groups. Instruct them that they should move into teams of no less than 4 and no more than 6. Give each group flip chart paper, and markers.

Read the following lead-in to the group:

"Gutters are designed to collect water running off of a house's roof and direct it towards a safe place. However, things other than water collect in gutters, such as leaves, fir needles, and pinecones, and can block the drainage pipes. If these are not removed from the gutter, the overflowing water can saturate the soil next to the home's foundation. This results in settling, which then causes the foundation to crack. The overflowing water also rots the wood in the roof next to the gutters, causing extensive damage.

A small business has its own gutters. The gutters are norms that help the business produce its products or services. However, problems within an organization can be similar to leaves, fir needles, and pinecones. If not resolved regularly, they can damage or destroy effectiveness.

Your assignment is to draw a visual representation of this analogy on the flip chart paper. At the center should be a picture that represents a small business. Draw pictures of behaviors that lead to cluttered gutters and behaviors that lead to clean gutters."

Give them a maximum of 10 minutes to complete their drawings. Have them explain their drawing.

Debrief Questions:
- ▶ How did your team decide on what the business should look like?
- ▶ What did it feel like to draw the behaviors?
- ▶ What does drawing pictures do as compared to just writing the words?
- ▶ How can this help you in the marketplace?

Awesome Tips:

Since it is a pictorial representation of beliefs and behaviors, and to make it a little tougher, have them use pictures only. No words.

Tech of Tomorrow

Purpose: To encourage your participants to think about technology and how it may effect their business in the future. The product development aspect allows them to be creative and resourceful.

Materials: Flip chart paper and markers for each team.

How to: Divide your class into small groups. Instruct them that they should move into teams of no less than 4 and no more than 6. Give each group flip chart paper, and markers.

Read the following lead-in to the group:

"Communication methods have changed drastically over the last fifty years. Most children today have no idea what a rotary phone looks like, let alone how to use one. We now have cell phones, text messages, e-mail, and instant messages. Social network sites dominate the internet. Just imagine how things will change in the future!

Your assignment is to create an all-new method of communication. You have 8 minutes to discuss and draw a device that people will use to communicate in the year 2050, and then 1 minute to present your invention to the rest of the group."

Give them time to work in their team to generate ideas, design and draw their invention. Be sure to let them know when there are 5 minutes and 3 minutes left on the clock, so they have time to finish their invention and plan for their presentation.

Each team should then present their invention to the rest of the group. Have the entire group vote on which invention is most feasible. Note: If the team is highly competitive, make it a rule that participants cannot vote for their team's idea.

Debrief
Questions: ▶ How creative were you in your invention?
▶ How do you think technology will affect your business in the future?
▶ What can you do to stay informed about advances in technology?

Awesome
Tips: Technology is changing every day and will affect everyone's business. A great example of this is the transition from VHS tapes to DVDs. In 1999, the majority of video sales were VHS tapes. At that time, even some experts in the industry did not foresee a big move to the new DVD format. However, within 5 years there was a complete switch, and DVDs dominated the market for movies sales and rentals.

Emphasize to your participants that technology can be a considerable help to them and their business. If they do not stay current with trends, it may eventually cause their demise.

Austin Cycles

Purpose: To consider what an ideal future would look like for their business, and to create and articulate a vision of what they can achieve.

Materials: Large sheets of paper and markers for each team.

How to: Divide your class into small groups. Instruct them that they should move into teams of no less than 4 and no more than 6. Give each group flip chart paper, and markers.

Read the following lead-in to the group:

"Louis Wilson has been the owner of Austin Cycles for 3 years. He's managed his team, kept costs under control, and put in place plans to reduce turnover and to train new employees. Things are going pretty well.

Although his team is performing, Louis feels that there is a lack of challenge and excitement. Louis believes that Austin Cycles could be the best-known, best-liked motorcycle dealer in Austin.

Your assignment is to help Louis 'paint a picture' of his vision for the future. Draw what might be happening in the stores. What would the customers see? What would staff be doing? How would everyone feel? What would the shopping experience be? Work with your team to develop a vision for Louis' team."

Debrief

Questions: ► What did it feel like to draw your vision?

► What does drawing pictures do as compared to just writing the words?

► How did your team decide on the vision and what it would look like?

► How can this help you in the marketplace?

Awesome

Tips: Since it is a pictorial representation of a vision for the future, and to make it a little tougher, have them use pictures only. No words.

Life Line

Purpose: To show participants that changes may seem to create problems, but they can always find ways to overcome them and be successful.

Materials: Paper and writing utensils.

How to: Give a pen and paper to each participant. Have them each remember five major changes they have experienced in their lifetimes. Instruct participants to draw timelines of their lives, and mark when each of the major changes occurred with an "X". Have the participants pair up. Ask them to share with their partner one of the major changes.

Post these questions for them to answer as they share:
- What made the change difficult?
- What was the key to your success in dealing with change?
- How did you feel before, during, and after the change?
- How were other things affecting your ability to deal with this change?

Debrief Questions:
- ▶ How did you feel sharing these experiences with each other?
- ▶ What did you learn from how your partner dealt with their major change?
- ▶ What did you learn about the compounding effect of changes that are close to each other?
- ▶ How can this help you in the marketplace?

Awesome
Tips: To be a successful entrepreneur your participants
             will have to walk through many changes. Realizing
             what they have done in the past when dealing with
             change, whether good or bad, can help them to deal
             with change in the future.

             Tell the participants that they will be asked to only
             share one of the major life changes they remember.
             Share only what is comfortable.

Clenched Fist

Purpose: To show that often times the easiest solution is overlooked for more complex choices.

Materials: None

How to: Start by asking the people in your class to partner with someone. After each person has found a partner, ask one person in the pair to be Partner A and the other person to be Partner B – they can choose which is which. Ask Partner A to clench their right fist as tight as they can. Tell Partner B it is their job to get that fist unclenched in 30 seconds.

You'll see people try all different strategies of force and guile. However, very few will think to just ask their partner to unclench their fist.

Debrief Questions:
- ▶ Was it difficult to get your partner's fist open?
- ▶ Did anyone think to simply ask?
- ▶ What are some ways we overlook the obvious in our everyday lives?
- ▶ In the marketplace?

Awesome Tips: In long trainings this is a great activity to use when you see energy waning. It gets everyone on their feet, gets people laughing and involved with each other, and all in less than 2 minutes. It's the perfect combination of illuminator and energizer!

Notes

Resist telling people how something should be done.
Instead, tell them what needs to be done.
They will often surprise you with creative solutions.
- Unknown

True North

Purpose: To quickly show the dynamics of leadership, communication, vision, mission statements, management skills and how things can go drastically wrong.

Materials: None

How to: Ask everyone in the room to stand to their feet. Have them extend their arms to the side so they are arms length away from any neighbor. They may have to move out into the aisles or take space in the front or back of the room. Ask them to raise their right hand high over their head and point with their fore finger. Now bring their right arm down so it is pointing straight out in front of them. Explain to them that their right arm is in essence the needle of a compass. In just a minute you are going to ask them to close their eyes and follow your instructions.

Say to them: "Everyone close your eyes and with your right arm as the needle of the compass I want you to turn your entire body and point in the direction that you believe to be true North." Emphasize that no one should open their eyes while they are turning to point in the direction of true North. After about 10 seconds make sure that everyone has completed the instructions and then ask them to open their eyes.

It is quickly evident that everyone is pointing in a different direction. Ask them, "What if this were the team that you were trying to get all going in one direction? Where would your team be?"

Now pick a spot in the room that everyone can easily see. The lighted EXIT signs over the door works well for this. With their eyes open ask everyone to point to that spot. The team is now all going in the same direction.

Debrief
Questions:
- ►Have you been on a team that looked like this?
- ►What happens when you don't ensure that everyone knows the objective?
- ►How important is clarity when achieving your desired outcomes?
- ►How can this help you in the marketplace?

Awesome
Tips:
This illuminator takes less than 2 minutes to complete and works for any size group large or small. They will remember the relevance of this exercise long after the training is over.

Contributed by Robert Mallon - www.rmallon.com

Hairy Knuckles

Purpose: To show that 2 people looking at the same thing can have different perspectives.

Materials: None

How to: Start by asking the people in your class to partner up with someone. After each person has found a partner, ask them to turn and face each other. Ask one of them to put up their hand between the two of them. Now ask them to describe to each other exactly what they see.

Be sure they give plenty of detail. For example: the length of life lines, the back of a ring, the big diamond, hairy knuckles, etc. As the partners look at the same hand they will be describing 2 different things because of their individual perspective – depending on which side of the hand they are on.

Debrief Questions:
► Is it possible for two people to look at the same thing, and see completely different things?
► Is one or the other right or wrong?
► What judgments do you make about others perceptions?
► Do you assume they're wrong, and you are right?
► How can this help you in the marketplace?

Awesome Tips: This activity is good for explaining how different types of people will see different things in your print ads, when looking at your products, when working on a project together, etc.

You can lead into a deeper discussion on:
- Different generations see things differently.
- Different genders see things differently.

Timing is Everything

Purpose: To illuminate the differences in people's perception of time.

Materials: Projector and screen.

How to: Project a digital clock onto your screen. Instruct your participants to stand and move if necessary to where they can easily see the clock on the screen. Tell them that when you direct them to, you want them to close their eyes and count to 60 as if they were counting 60 seconds off a clock. When they reach 60 they should open their eyes and raise their hand, and look at the time on the screen – but not to make any other movements or sounds.

Debrief Questions:
- ►Was it evident that everyone had a different concept of time?
- ►What does this show us about peoples concept of time?
- ►Do you know people who are always late?
- ►Could their concept of time play into that?
- ►How can this help you in the marketplace?

Awesome Tips: This quick exercise is a great illuminator into individual concepts of time. What you'll experience is that people's perception of 60 seconds usually ranges anywhere from 35 seconds to 2 minutes.

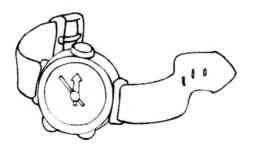

Tear it Up

Purpose: To emphasize the need for clarity when speaking, and the need for listening when being spoken to.

Materials: Paper.

How to: Depending on your group size you can give everyone a blank piece of paper or you can ask for 5-7 volunteers to come to the front of the room. Then ask them to close their eyes and follow your directions. Tell them that they are not to ask any questions during the instructional phase.

Give the following directions. First, fold the sheet in half. Then fold it in half again. Now fold it in half yet again. Tear off the right-hand corner. Turn the sheet over and tear off the left-hand corner.

Now get the participants to open their eyes and unfold their sheets of paper. It is immediately apparent that the group does not have identically finished products. With the right questions this now leads into a discussion about how to improve communication skills, management by objectives, following instructions, listening skills, or giving directions.

Debrief Questions:
- ▶ Did everyone's paper come out the same?
- ▶ Why or Why not?
- ▶ How important are the details when giving and receiving instructions?
- ▶ How can this help you in the marketplace?

**Awesome
Tips:**   Intentionally do not answer questions when giving
              instructions. The point of the exercise is for the
              papers to come out different to emphasize the need
              for clarity.

80/20

Purpose: This activity can be used in an endless number of situations. Use your debrief time to magnify the truth of the Pareto Principle.

Materials: Paper and writing utensils.

How to: Give each participant a piece of paper and a writing utensil.

Next read these instructions to them. Make sure that you give them time to do the calculations:

"Think of a number between 1 and 10 and write it down. Now multiply that number times 9. You should have gotten 2 digits in your answer ... I want you to add those 2 digits together. Now subtract 5. Translate that new number to a letter of the alphabet .. for example 1= A, 2 = B, 3 = C, 4 = D, 5 = E, etc. Now think of a country that begins with that letter and write it down. Look at the country you just wrote and pick out the second letter of that country. Now think of an animal that begins with that letter and write it down." Now ask ... "How many of you are writing an elephant in Denmark?"

This is a classic example of Pareto's 80/20 principle. 80% of the class wrote an elephant in Denmark. The remaining 20% wrote either an Elk or Emu in Denmark, or perhaps, an Ostrich in the Dominican Republic. You can explain that it was an Italian economist Vilfredo Pareto, who in the 1870's determined that 80% of Italy's wealth was controlled by 20% of the population.

Go on to give them more 80/20 examples, such as these common rules of thumb in business:
- 80% of your sales come from 20% of your clients
- 80% of your sales come from 20% of your advertising
- 20% of your stock takes up 80% of your warehouse
- 20% of your staff will cause 80% of your problems

Debrief Questions:
► How much of your day is spent on trivial tasks?
► When was the last time you checked your web traffic logs?
► Which key words are bringing you the most traffic?
► Have you identified which of your ads pull the most?
► How can this help you in the marketplace?

Awesome Tips:
At first everyone will think that you were able to read their minds. You can choose to explain your magic trick or not. (*Any number multiplied by 9, when you add the digits together they will equal 9. You easily led them through your multiplication and subtraction, where you wanted them to go.*)

Reach For The Sky

Purpose: To show participants with a quick illustration that even when we think we're doing our very best, we can usually do just a little bit better.

Materials: None

How to: In discussion about time management, or managing employees, or wherever appropriate – do a proper set up to this exercise by asking the question. "Have you ever found that people most times think they are doing the very best they can? If you agree with that, please raise your hand as high as you can so that I can see it."

Hands will go up across the audience. Remember, you asked them to raise their hand as high as they could. Now stop for just a second or two. Look at everyone and say – "OK, now raise your hand a little higher." *You'll see everyone's hands go up just a little bit more. Smile and ask them, "Didn't I ask you to raise your hand as high as you can the first time? How come you were able to raise it higher?"*

Debrief Questions:
- ►Have you ever needed just a little more from someone?
- ►How willing were they to help?
- ►Does it vary from person to person?
- ►What are some good ways to get that extra 10%?
- ►How can this help you in the marketplace?

Awesome
Tips:

It helps to demonstrate this activity from the front of the room. As you ask them to raise their hands, raise your hand also, so they have someone to mirror. Chances are they will raise their hand only as high as you raise yours, so when you ask them to raise theirs, be sure not to "reach for the sky".

$20 Bill

Purpose: To quickly demonstrate the concept of self-esteem, self-worth and personal value. It causes your participants to consider whether they take responsibility for their own actions and emotional well-being and quickly illuminates how they handle tough circumstances.

Materials: $20 Bill

How to: Pull a $20 bill out of your pocket or wallet and say this: "Suppose I told you that at the end of training today that I am going to stand at the door and that I plan to give this $20 to one person. How many of you would be a willing recipient of this $20 bill?"

Not everyone will raise their hand, so then say: "I noticed that some of you did not raise your hand and I guess that can be for one of two reasons. *One, you have so much money to burn that you don't need my $20 bill. Or two, you're wondering, 'What's the catch?' That's because people have violated your trust in the past.* You don't even know me yet, and you're not sure if you can trust me. I'm going to ask you to play along – there are no strings attached. So let me ask again, how many of you would be a willing recipient of this $20 bill?"

Now, take the $20 bill and crinkle it up into a small ball, and ask: "How many of you would take the $20 bill in this condition?"

Next, throw the $20 bill onto the ground a couple times. Leave the bill lying on the floor and ask:

"How many of you would still want the $20 bill?"

Finally, kick the bill around on the floor, stomp on it, jump up and down on it, and then pick the smashed bill up by just a corner and ask: "How many of you would still take it?"

Most people will still raise their hands, so ask them: "I've abused this money ... squeezed it, smashed it, thrown it on the ground, kicked it around, stomped on it ... why would you still want it?"

You'll get answers such as: "Because it's still a $20 bill." ... and ... "Because it hasn't lost its value."

Open the bill and ask them: "Do you agree that you as a human being have more value than this piece of paper? Even if you've been mistreated, have you lost your value? Many of you have been squeezed, smashed, kicked around, stomped on ... and you believe that your value is less today."

Debrief
Questions: ▶ What kinds of things squeeze you in your business?
▶ How many of you don't feel valued in your business?
▶ Does anyone ever tell you that you're valuable?
▶ When was the last time you told someone how valuable they are to you?

Awesome
Tips: This is a powerful opportunity for you to share how your organization can help them with solutions when they are feeling squeezed in their business. Encourage them to stay plugged in and to use your center as a resource. Remind them that you and your team value them as individuals.

Contributed by Keith New of HQ Solutions - www.hqsolutions.biz

Software Trainer

Purpose: To offer a relevant case study that applies an element of realism. This helps the participants identify their attitudes about the topic, and work together to apply problem-solving skills.

Materials: One copy of the adjacent page per participant.

How to: Ask your participants to find a partner to work with during this exercise. Distribute the printed case study and tell them: "Read the following situation, and work with your partner to identify at least 3 things that went wrong during this training session."

Debrief Questions:
- ▶ What adult learning concepts did the software trainer violate?
- ▶ What causes trainers to teach in this manner?
- ▶ What are some training concepts you want to be sure to incorporate into your training sessions?

Awesome Tips: The end result of case studies is to provide a note of realism while boosting the rate of learning. Given a case study, and using their own experiences, the participants will be able to identify what went wrong and plan how to make adjustments in their own training sessions.

Software Trainer Case Study

An accounting software trainer began his training session by announcing his objective:

"I will explain how the accounting system works, how to navigate the software, and how I usually troubleshoot problems with journal entries." He then darkened the room and proceeded to show a series of slides that paralleled his lecture. He frequently read to the group directly from the slides.

Participants were given handout materials that showed three slides per page to use for taking notes. They were asked to hold their questions until the end of the session. The trainer added "Most of your questions will be answered during the training. So please be patient." The trainer showed about 40 slides during the first hour of the lecture.

What's wrong here?

Sweet Spot

Purpose: To demonstrate to your participants the importance of identifying their target niche to conduct realistic market research.

Materials: White board or flip chart and a marker.

How to: Tell your participants that you are looking for some volunteers to help you demonstrate how to determine a niche market. Warn them that you may be a little tough on them, but that they will learn very valuable information about their niche market.

People will be more than willing to volunteer. Write their type of business on the board or flip chart. For example participants may say things like, A Doggy Day Care, Personal Trainer, "Green" Cleaning Products, or Web Development. Pick one from the list that you know most people in the class will have a general understanding of how the business works.

Ask the person who volunteered the business to list the characteristics of their ideal customer and write these on the board or flip chart.

Explain to the group that you are going to find the Sweet Spot for this business. The Sweet Spot is like the bulls eye of a target. Teach them the concepts of identifying the 3 "graphics":
Demographics: Who they are?
Geographics: Where they are?
Psychographics: Why they buy?

Now go back to the list that you just wrote on the

board, and ask the group: "How have we done in identifying the Sweet Spot? Are any of our categories too broad? Are there more characteristics that are important that we haven't listed here?" *Use this as an opportunity to lead into a more in depth instruction on the importance of having a clearly defined niche.*

After your teaching, if time permits, go back and pick a second business to use as an example. This time the class should do a little better on defining the Sweet Spot.

Debrief
Questions: ▶ Who are your customers?
                  ▶ Where are they? Why do they buy?
                  ▶ What can you do with this information to help you develop a marketing strategy?

Awesome
Tip: Be sure to thank the volunteers for being so willing to share their business information. You can jokingly tell the class that they should forward their bill for conducting this valuable market research directly to the volunteer.

T-Chart

Purpose: To use guided note taking as a set up for the concepts that you want to teach in the training session.

Materials: White board or flip chart and a marker.

How To: Draw a T-Chart on the board or flip chart. Write any topic headings that you want to use on the chart. For example:

Do Delegate	Don't Delegate
Good Customer Service	Bad Customer Service
Feedback Do's	Feedback Don'ts
Good Activities	Bad Activities
Passive	Aggressive
Negotiating Do's	Negotiating Don'ts

Ask your participants to give you examples and record their answers on the proper sides of the T-Chart. Use the list you have generated to lead into the information that you are planning to teach.

Debrief Questions:
- ►What experiences have you had like this?
- ►How do you feel when _____ happens? (Choose something from either side.)
- ►How will you do things differently in the future?
- ►How can you use this information to train your team?

Awesome
Tips: T-Charts can be used for any topic that you are
                   teaching. They are especially helpful in situations
                   where you have had limited activity preparation
                   time.

SWOT Analysis

Purpose: To teach your participants how to do a SWOT Analysis for their business.

Materials: White board or flip chart and a marker.

How to: Draw a SWOT chart on the board or flip chart. Ask your participants to draw an identical chart for themselves to use.

Strengths	Weaknesses
Opportunities	Threats

Explain to your participants how to evaluate the internal _Strengths_ and _Weaknesses_ of their business, and the external _Opportunities_ and _Threats_ that exist. Ask them to write examples in each of the four squares.

Give them about 5 minutes to think of items that should be included in their chart. Then ask them to partner with someone to review their business and the items they wrote on their SWOT chart. Ask the partners to help each other identify any additional items to include on the chart.

Debrief
Questions: ▶ How tough was it to identify the Weaknesses and Threats?
▶ What can you do to compensate for those areas?
▶ How can you capitalize on the Strengths and Opportunities?
▶ How can this help you in the marketplace?

Awesome
Tip: Tell your class that when conducting a SWOT analysis that they should be brutally honest with themselves. This is not the time to gloss over any areas. It is better to identify the weaknesses and threats that exist for their business so that they can realistically adopt a strategy to overcome them.

Conflict Consensus

Purpose: To practice proper communication when dealing with conflicting opinions.

Materials: One copy of the adjacent page per participant.

How to: Ask participants to partner up. Distribute the conflict management form to each person. Have participants attempt to match up each of the words in the left column with the correct definition in the right column. They can use each word only once.

Participants must come to a complete agreement with their partner for matching all ten words. Once they agree, they must go find another pair of participants, and come to 100% agreement with them. Those four participants will then go to another group of four and discuss until they agree. Continue this doubling procedure until the entire class can agree on all ten words.

Debrief
Questions:
▶ Did anyone at any point get upset? Frustrated?
▶ Were there any instances where you thought you knew better than everyone else?
▶ How did you overcome conflicting opinions?
▶ How can this help you in the marketplace?

Awesome
Tips: At the end of the activity, be sure to inform them that the definitions were intentionally vague. There are no definite answers, just as many times there are no definite answers in the real world. This will also settle any upset die-hards who were certain they were correct.

Conflict Management Tools

Match the words in the left column with the correct phrase in the right column. Each word in the left column may only be used one time.

1. Sharing   _____ Telling the truth, avoiding deceit

2. Vulnerability   _____ Differences and unique characteristics

3. Loyalty   _____ Willingness to exchange ideas and
                               ideals with others

4. Accepting others   _____ Willingness to explore new
                               experiences

5. Involving others   _____ Important information, personal
                               events, and prior experiences

6. Valuing   _____ Commitment to the goals of the team
                               and its mission

7. Awareness   _____ Asking others for their ideas, input,
                               and feedback

8. Communication   _____ Willingness to have both strengths and
                               weaknesses known by others

9. Openness   _____ Sensitivity to the needs and
                               perceptions of others

10. Honesty   _____ Expressing oneself clearly, both
                               orally and in writing

Contributed by Irene Maxfield

Next Level Development

Purpose: To demonstrate the importance of planning and to encourage your participants to take the next steps necessary in their business.

Materials: Make enough copies of the Next Level Development Plan for everyone in your seminar.

How to: Give a brief introduction on why it is important to have a development plan. A plan is a road map to future success and can be used to evaluate progress on the road to where you are going. The key elements in the Next Level Plan should include: 1) the results desired, 2) the minimum acceptable standard, 3) a target date, and 4) specific action steps to be taken to achieve the stated goals.

Encourage the participants to write action steps that can be completed and checked off. For example, "Develop a Marketing Plan" is not an action step, it is a goal. An action step is "Find the trade associations and their websites for my industry."

After you have introduced the concept of planning, and the difference between goals and action steps, distribute the forms to your seminar participants. Guide them through the steps to complete the plan.

Give them at least 10 minutes to complete the form. Then have them work with a partner to identify one short-term goal and the action steps they have written for achieving that goal.

Debrief

Questions: ▶ How difficult was it to write your short- and long-term goals?

▶ **Can** your action steps be completed and checked off?

▶ How difficult was it to share your goals and action steps with your partner?

▶ Do you believe that you will be able to achieve your goals?

Awesome

Tips: The Next Level Development Plan can also be introduced in management training seminars. Your participants can use it to evaluate one of their employees and develop a Next Level Plan with them. It is not a formal performance appraisal, rather a form to be used to help coach people to the next level.

When your participants identify the training they need to support their development areas, be sure to promote your center's upcoming training sessions and other ways that you can help them fill that need.

Next Level Development Plan

Name: _____ Date: _____

Strengths: _____
_____
_____

Areas for development: _____
_____
_____

Training to support development needs:
_____
_____
_____

Short-term goals: _____
_____
_____

Actions steps to attain short-term goals:
_____
_____
_____

Long-term goals: _____
_____
_____

Actions steps to attain short-term goals:
_____
_____
_____

Section 4

When All Else Fails ...
Have Fun!

When All Else Fails ... Have Fun

1. **Approach every training session with curiosity.** Expect surprise and wonder.

2. **Don't be intimidated by challenges.** They are learning opportunities for you and everyone else, so handle with grace.

3. **Practice the Circle of Success.** To be a success, make the people around you successful. Once you put it into motion, the circle keeps turning, bringing success back to you as you help others.

4. **Let your students see the enthusiasm you have for your subject and your love of learning.** Your enthusiasm will be contagious

5. **Finally, remember that a ship in the harbor is safe, but that is not what ships are built for.** Take a chance; try new things; get out of your comfort zone.

Relay

Purpose: To develop team building, open communication within teams, and introduce and apply synergy.

Materials: 2-3 packs of playing cards and a stopwatch.

How to: Based on the number of people in your room, you will need to figure out how to divide them into groups with the exact same amount of people. You want no less than 5 per group, and no more than 8. If you have people left over after dividing up the teams, ask them to help you as referees or timers. Count out 26 cards for each team. Move the people into their teams. Give each team one stack of cards. Tell them this is a card passing competition.

The players at one end of each line must take one card at a time off the pile of cards and pass it to the team member sitting next to them. That team member then passes the card on to the third team member, and so on. When the final team member receives a card they must place it in a pile next to them. When the last person on the team discards the last card, they should yell, "Done!" The timer will yell a time back to them. There are 5 basic rules:

1. You must stay in your seat.
2. Cards start in a stack and end in a stack.
3. You can only have one card in your possession at a time.
4. Every team member must touch every card.
5. If a team member drops a card the rest of the team must wait until the card has been picked up again before continuing.

Teams will go through a preliminary round with no planning. Announce everyone's times to the whole group. They will then have a few minutes to plan their strategies before starting the final round. The 5 basic rules still apply, but anything else they want to change they may.

After giving them a few minutes to plan, ask them to get ready to start again. The team with the fastest time is declared the winner

Debrief Questions:
- ► How did the winning team win?
- ► Who led the planning session? Why?
- ► Was the planning stage of any value to the groups? Why?
- ► How can this help you in the marketplace?

Awesome Tips:
Recommended for smaller groups (less than 50). This activity is fun, but can get loud. You can also announce previous "record times" for groups of the same capacity as a motivator for them to improve.

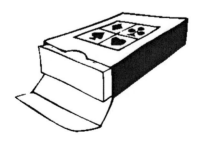

Rain Makers

Purpose: To emphasizes creativity, teamwork, and working with different personality types.

Materials: None

How to: Divide your class into small groups. Instruct them that they should move into teams of no less than 4 and no more than 6.

Read the following lead-in to the group:

"A machine requires that each part be involved with at least one other part at least some of the time. In your groups, you have five minutes to devise a book printing machine, which you'll present to the other groups. Every member of your team must be a '*part*' of the machine."

Have the groups present their machines. Once they have finished, with the same groups, ask them to make a machine that makes rain. Give them another 5 minutes, then present the machines. Lastly ask them to devise a machine that makes happiness. Give them 5 more minutes and present the machines.

Debrief Questions:
▶ Which machines that you have just seen did you admire the most and why?
▶ What made those machines successful?
▶ What was the best balance between discussing it and trying it?
▶ Could you work together on this activity entirely without talking?

Awesome
Tips: You can use any sequence from physical products,
(belt, tofu, shoelaces) to less machine-like products,
(wind, dancing, homerun) to abstract products
(love, telekinesis, taste, etc.). Such sequencing
encourages increased creativity and imagination,
and stretches the group further into improvisational
territory.

Paper Airplanes

Purpose: To help participants with problem solving and get creative ideas for dealing with work issues.

Materials: Paper and writing utensils.

How to: Each participant writes their name and one problem or concern they currently face on a piece of paper. Give the group 2 minutes to do this. Have everyone make an airplane with their piece of paper.

Divide the room in half, and ask one of the groups to fly their planes. The second group should pick up a plane and find the person who it belongs to. They then have 3-5 minutes to work together to solve that problem.

When time is up, have the other half of the room fly their planes and repeat the process.

Debrief Questions:
- ►How many got one or more ideas that will truly help them resolve their issue?
- ►How did you feel about having to give advice?
- ►Why do we not ask each other for help more often?
- ►How can this help you in the marketplace?

Awesome Tips: Encourage partial advice, rather than no advice. Even if you don't know the answer to their problem, ask your partner questions and strategize on possible solutions.

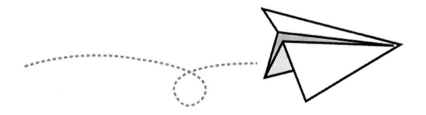

Linked Together

Purpose: To develop team building, and introduce the importance of planning.

Materials: A small box of paper clips for each team.

How to: Divide your class into small groups. Instruct them that they should move into teams of no less than 4 and no more than 6.

Give each team a box of paper clips and tell them that they have 3 minutes to make a chain of paper clips as long as possible. All team members must be involved in the process of making the chain. But here's the catch — all team members must place one hand behind their back, and only use one hand while helping to make the chain!

Do not give the teams a lot of time to prepare for this. Simply give them the instructions and then tell them to start. At the end of 3 minutes say "Stop!" and ask each team to count the number of clips in their link.

Give them a few minutes to strategize with their team on how they can increase the number of clips in their link. Remind them that everyone on the team must be involved in the construction of the chain in some way. After giving them a few minutes to plan, ask them to disassemble the paper clip chain and get ready to start again.

Tell them to start again and at the end of 3 minutes say "Stop!" Ask each team to count the number of clips in their link.

The team with the most paper clips in their chain is declared the winner!

Debrief Questions:

▶ What is this exercise really about?

▶ How did the different personalities on the team affect your process?

▶ What did you do differently the second time?

▶ How can this help you in the marketplace?

Awesome Tips:

What a fun way to get people moving! Plus this activity can lead into a wide variety of training topics: planning, communication, delegation, team work, process improvement, personality styles, and more!

Vogue

Purpose: To show participants the importance of clearly understanding the desired outcome before starting or delegating a task.

Materials: Index cards, a marker and basket. Prizes.

How to: Write the following on the index cards: dancing, reading, eating, talking on the phone, skiing, swimming, playing football, surfing, digging a hole, watching TV, flying, and sleeping. Fold the index cards in half and place them in the basket.

It is best to use this activity in groups of no more than 24. You can make it into a competition by dividing the class into 2 teams. Each team will then try to guess the activity being portrayed and whichever team guesses first, wins that round. You can keep score and award the winning team a small prize.

Read the following instructions to your group:
"Please find a partner. Decide between the two of you who will be Partner A and who will be Partner B. In this basket are a number of index cards. Each card has an activity written on it. Partner A will chose a card from the basket and read it to yourself. Do not say aloud the word on your card. You are to then move your Partner into the pose that conveys that activity.

It is OK to gesture, tell, or show your partner how to move, but you cannot tell them what the end result is supposed to be.

The rest of the participants will try to guess the activity portrayed.

After the activity is guessed, repeat steps 3, 4 and 5 with a new set of partners, until everyone has had the chance to participate.

Debrief Questions:
▶ Partner A – how did it feel to give instructions without knowing what the outcome should be?
▶ Partner B – what part of the instructions did you have a difficult time following?
▶ How could you have been more effective?
▶ How can this help you in the marketplace?

Awesome Tips:
The activity can be used as an energizer after a couple hours of training. It gets everyone on their feet and gives people the opportunity to laugh together. Be sure to introduce the concept of how to achieve desired outcomes before you start the activity and then lead into additional relevant information following your debrief.

It's a Circus

Purpose: To improve communication and market strategies.

Materials: One long balloon, like clowns use, for each participant — plus some extras. A balloon pump is optional, but recommended.

How to: Divide your class into small groups. Instruct them that they should move into teams of no less than 4 and no more than 6.

Give each participant one balloon. Have each team create a useful balloon structure that they will attempt to market. The individuals balloons may be joined or independent.

Give them 8 minutes to build their sculpture, then have them share their creation with the class. They should identify what the product is, what it is used for, and who would be interested in buying it.

Debrief Questions:
► Was it difficult to come up with a product using balloons?
► How did you deal with everyone's ideas for the sculpture?
► How did you handle disagreements?

Awesome Tips: Have the balloons blown up prior to the activity if possible. You can ask the early arrivers to your class to help you if they'd like. This is a great icebreaker in itself.

Do not inflate the balloons all the way. Leave an inch or two to avoid popping while bending and twisting. Have extra balloons ready.

Listen and Learn

**Use the Totally Awesome Training CD and
Activity Guide to Boost Your Presentation Skills**

1. **Break it up.** Listen to the Totally Awesome Training Audio
   CD in intervals of 8-10 minutes. Then, stop the CD so that
   you can process the information that you heard, and, most
   importantly, apply it to your training regimen.

2. **Listen to the CD several times.** As an adult learner, you
   need to hear something at least 6 times to really learn it.
   You'll get awesome new ideas each time you listen to the
   CD.

3. **Tell someone what you've learned.** Did you know that you
   will retain ideas differently when you teach them to someone
   else?

4. **Use the Totally Awesome Training Activity Guide.** It will
   help you develop and bring activities into your training room.

5. **Go online to www.entreprenowonline.com.** Download additional free tips and tools and begin delivering totally awesome training.

Game On!

Discover the What and Why of Putting Gamification to Work

Game On! Discover the What and Why of Putting Gamification to Work

Chapter 1—

Game On

My adventure into the world of Gamification began in the summer of 2012 when I received a call from a client asking me to develop a Gamification Workshop to teach problem solving skills. I was honored to be asked and thanked her for thinking of me.

I assured her that I was the ideal professional trainer to hire for this workshop ... after all, I have earned a reputation for using games to interact and motivate participants in all my leadership, strategic thinking, and communication workshops.

However, as I asked her about her objectives and outcome goals, I was quickly Googling the word "Gamification." Truth was, at the time, I didn't have a clue what Gamification was. I had heard the term bantered around, but it wasn't anything I had turned my focus to.

Fortunately, the first article I stumbled upon was by Adam Carstens and John Beck called "Get Ready for the Gamer Generation." (TechTrends, 2005)

What I read started to change my entire way of thinking about the Gamer Generation and games in the workplace.

I sat fascinated while watching a TED talk given by Californian game designer, Jane McGonigal. She says that by the time they turn 21, a dedicated gamer will spend 10,000 hours playing video games – exactly the amount of time they will have spent in formal education.

According to McGonigal, four miraculous things happen to

gamers while playing during those 10,000 hours.

- First, they become urgently optimistic, over-whelmed by a desire to win.

- Second, they bond closely together since those who play together are more inclined to like and trust each other.

- Third, it makes them happy over-achievers, sitting at their screens for hours in a state of focused bliss.

- And finally, it furnishes them with some sort of epic purpose – a larger-than-life reason for being.

What interests me about these four states is that they are precisely the things that make up a model employee – an optimistic, idealistic team worker who is blissfully happy to create, innovate, and work away all day and all night.

Indeed, if only some way could be found to make the working world a bit more like World of Warcraft, then not only would offices vanish, so would all problems of morale, lack of engagement, and slackers.

But before I got too carried away with this high-tech nirvana, a couple of other things occurred to me. From observing the excessive gaming that went on in our recreation room as my sons grew up, I also remembered that video games make people lazy, grumpy, and addicted to instant gratification.

They also make you terribly inefficient: You feel productive while achieving nothing. They make you think you can do things you can't, like be a global ruler or throw touchdowns like Tom Brady when you are actually not in shape enough to run round the block.

Then again, don't we see those same traits from some of the Boomers in our working world -- inefficiency, laziness, and overconfidence?

Maybe the new version of the workplace, run by the Gaming Generation, won't be that different after all.

But, this is not a guide about video games or the games industry.

This guide is about how you can use Gamification to improve your business practices. Gamification is a powerful tool in your leadership and management toolbox. You can apply it to your existing business challenges, whatever type of organization you are in.

Because many people feel motivated by well-designed game features, monetary rewards aren't always necessary, the game itself is the reward. For example, gamers invest enormous resources into acquiring virtual objects and achievements that have no tangible value.

Games are great practice for real life. Specifically, they are a good training environment in organizations where collaborative problem solving is an essential element in how work gets done. The world of games, which looks like a ridiculous waste of time to many in the Boomer Generation, turns out to be a valuable boot camp for the future of business.

So for the moment, can you suspend disbelief with me, and enter the world of games and the G Generation? For the time being, put away any thoughts that sound like, "It's time to grow up and put the games away. We are important people doing important work!"

This guide is your opportunity to experience how Gamification can transform your organization and serve your clients.

Gamification is an important and powerful new strategy for influencing and motivating people.

Forward thinking organizations everywhere are beginning to understand the power of Gamification to increase engagement, as well as the bottom line, and are quickly learning how to leverage its power. Let's enter the world of Gamification together.

Game On!

Chapter 2—

What is Gamification?

What's the Buzz?

Gamification is a buzz word used to describe systems that take elements of games and apply them to everyday life. Perhaps the best-known example of Gamification is Four-square, the location-based social network in which people "check in" to places via their phones. Users are awarded badges for going out and experiencing new things. And the more they frequent a place, the higher their status becomes. They may become the "mayor" of their coffee shop, potentially opening the door to discounts and other prizes.

Gabe Zichermann – a prominent advocate of Gamification – defines it like this: *"Gamification is using game-based mechanics, aesthetics, and game thinking to engage people, motivate action, promote learning, and solve problems."*

Gamification is an important and powerful new strategy for influencing and motivating people. Simply defined, Gamification uses game mechanics and rewards for non-game applications in order to increase engagement and loyalty.

Forward thinking organizations are beginning to understand how the power of Gamification can increase engagement as well as the bottom line. They are quickly learning how to leverage its power. The business community is starting to realize the power Gamification has to build loyalty, improve customer and employee engagement, and incentivize employees and partners to perform at higher levels.

The term, "Gamification" first appeared on Google Trends in September 2010. It is currently a $100 million a year industry, expected to swell to $2.8 billion by 2015. With a trend like this, should your organization consider Gamification for it's training efforts?

Gamification Simplified

Gamification is the use of game elements and game-design techniques in non-game contexts. Let me break that down:

Game Elements: Think of game elements as a toolkit for building a game. Game elements include game pieces, avatars, rules, scoring points, proceeding to the next level, receiving badges, or unlocking a reward. As you begin to gamify a system, you should modify the elements to target certain business objectives, and to make the experience more engaging.

Game Techniques: The aspects of games that make them fun, addicting, and challenging can't be reduced to a list of components or step-by-step instructions. This is where game-design techniques come in. How do you decide which game elements to use to create a productive gamified experience? Just like strategic leadership, managing a team, or creating a killer marketing campaign, game design is a strong mix of knowledge, skill, and luck.

Non-game Context: The final aspect of our definition is that Gamification operates in non-game contexts such as on-boarding, marketing, training, client engagement, etc. The key element in each is that they involve real-world business goals. Your players are not storming a fortress, they are exploring the website of your new product. They are not collecting gold coins, they are collecting achievements on the way to learning a new skill or process in the workplace.

The three major non-game contexts are internal, external, and behavior change.

- Internal Gamification means that companies can use Gamification to improve productivity within the organization in order to encourage innovation, enhance teamwork, or otherwise obtain positive business results through their own employees. The motivational dynamics of Gamification must interact with the firm's existing management and reward structures.

- External Gamification involves your customers or prospective clients, members, or donors. These applications are generally driven by marketing objectives. Gamification here is a way to improve the relationships between businesses and customers, producing increased engagement, identification with the product, stronger loyalty, and ultimately higher revenues.

- Behavior-change Gamification seeks to form beneficial new habits among a population. It can involve anything from encouraging people to make better health choices (such as eating healthier or exercising more), to redesigning the classroom to make kids learn more while actually enjoying school. Generally, these new habits produce desirable community outcomes: less obesity, lower medical costs, or a more effective educational system.

In this guide we are focusing on internal Gamification, although we will reference examples of external and behavior -change contexts.

Welcome to the Real World
The challenge of Gamification, therefore, is to take the elements that normally operate within a game space and apply them effectively in the real world.

Gamification of real-world activities represents a powerful technique which can motivate people, differentiate an organization from other similar organizations, and help generate loyalty to the organization, its products, or its messages. There are a variety of ways Gamification of real-world activities motivate, including:

> **Engagement** - When challenged and rewarded, people are naturally motivated to engage more directly and intensely with information or activities.

> **Competition** – A sales leaderboard represents a Gamification mechanic that can help motivate people to move up, or stay on top, by selling more. Gamification elements that generate competition can act as powerful motivators.

> **Progression** – The inclusion of a progress bar linked to a simple set of tasks, such as completing training, frequently results in an immediate improvement in progress toward a real-world goal. By using gaming mechanics such as badges or 'leveling up,' people are often motivated to strive for higher levels of achievement.

> **Habit Formation** – Once a pattern is established, people are more often motivated by the reward to engage in activity as a preprogrammed response.

What it Means for Your Workplace
Let's look at a few of the characteristics of games that can be used in the workplace to engage and motivate employees, clients, and members.

Rajat Paharia, the founding father of Gamification, and the founder of the company Bunchball, realized that you could take the mechanics that game designers had been using for years, such as competition, real-time feedback, and goal-setting, and apply them elsewhere. He believes, "Outside of gaming, [game mechanics] still work to drive behavior because they are based on satisfying fundamental human needs and desires."

Real-Time Feedback: In a game, you receive instant feedback anytime you take an action. Good behavior is reinforced with positive feedback. Any negative feedback you receive enables you to learn quickly and adjust.

> **What it means for the workplace:** To accelerate growth and learning in new employees, clients, and members, organizations need systems and processes that enable fast and meaningful feedback.

Transparency: Games are a statistical nirvana – progress is tracked and communicated in real-time. Players can see exactly where they stand in relation to everyone else.

> **What it means for the workplace:** Everyone wants to know how they are doing. If they don't understand how performance is being measured, or how they are being compared to others, they can't make necessary adjustments to improve. Organizations need a way to capture data to share with employees in an easily understood format.

On-boarding and Mastery: Games don't just drop you into the middle of the action with no instruction on how to play. You'll never see or hear, "read the manual." Instead, games have mastered the process of on-boarding users—teaching them how to play from within the game itself. Players get live experience at "doing," coached by the system, until they have enough confidence and mastery to venture off on their own.

Farmville is a great example—it's a social game that looks simple, but it has Farm Coins, Farm Cash, Ribbons, Levels, Planting, Harvesting, and more. If you were dropped into the game with nothing but a plot of farmland, you would have no idea how to play or what to do first. Instead they teach you how to play by actually playing.

> **What it means for the workplace:** Organizations that can use the on-boarding and mastery techniques from games to drive ongoing engagement, will see benefits in both commitment and the bottom line.

Let's Go Play

Face it, we have been playing games since the days of the cavemen, and it is human nature to compare ourselves to others to see how we measure up. Many people are intensely competitive in games, trying to outpace and outsmart their way to the top.

Add technology to the mix, and today gaming has become a hugely popular and tremendously profitable industry, to the order of $60 billion per year.

The reality is:
- People enjoy playing games
- Popular games inspire extreme loyalty
- People are motivated by gaming reward and achievement systems
- Therefore, if non-games are made more game-like, we'll be more likely to 'play' them

Given this broad acceptance of gaming and the wide use of the internet, people have become more open to game mechanics in other parts of their lives. As a result, Gamification is becoming a powerful tool through which organizations teach, persuade, and motivate people.

The success of social networks and social gaming has demonstrated how behavioral psychology plays a factor in a successful user experience. Games have proven that people crave personal progress in building social connections and completing goals, especially in light of the fact that millions of people engage with these services without getting a dime in return.

At its core, Gamification is about finding the fun in the things that we have to do. Making business processes compelling by making them fun is about the most fascinating and coolest thing that I can think of!

Chapter 3—

The G Generation

Meet the Gamer or G Generation
There is a new generation of workers taking over key positions in your organization and in your classrooms. This generation is younger, yes, but they're also different in ways that will definitely change how business is done.

The way they spent their formative years has given them an entirely different set of skills from their parents or older co-workers – those differences are driven by one central factor: **The G Generation grew up playing video games.**

The G Generation – over 56 million strong – is a combination of Gen Xers (born between 1965 and 1981) and the Millennials (born since 1982).

Most of The G Generation is old enough to be in the workforce and they will soon outnumber their older bosses and co-workers. Before long, their way of thinking will pass the tipping point and become standard operating procedure in business.

And the Boomers (born between 1946 and 1964), who grew up without video games, will have to understand the gamers. That means not only learning what they're all about, but finding ways to redesign organizational onboarding, engagement, training, and even how work is done.

If that sounds unlikely or unreasonable, you may — like me and many people — have not realized the influence that video games have inserted into all areas of our culture.

Games are not a "niche" anymore. Americans now spend more money on video games each year than they do going to the movies, and more time at home playing video games than watching rented movies.

Today, about half of all Americans play video games. According to an International Game Developers Association (IGDA) study, the U.S. game industry alone does over $10 billion worth of sales annually. Some 92% of American kids from age 2 to 17 have regular access to video games; 80% live in households with PCs, and the Sony Playstation is in 25% of all US homes.

But to those outside the video game industry, most still view them as a child's toy – something to be put away or grown out of as they enter the workforce.

But many of your co-workers, staff, clients, or association members will tell you that some of their most important childhood memories center around playing these games. They have spent countless dollars and endless hours in the virtual worlds created by these toys.

Unlike television with its one-way communication, games are powerfully interactive and reinforce a myriad of behaviors. This has created entirely new ways of looking at the world and how it operates — and as a result, demands new and different delivery systems for learning, interacting, and long-term engagement.

Research into the development of the brain has shown early childhood and adolescence are the critical years for how the brain is prepared for perceiving and reacting to the world. These critical years leave our brains with a particular set of assumptions and beliefs about how the world works.

Games reinforce certain beliefs about the players themselves, how the world should work, how people relate to one another, and about the purpose of life in general.

Games create a self-centered universe where the player is in charge, and within certain rules or boundaries, can manipulate other people and objects.

Data from the Kaiser Family Foundation shows that an average 8-10 year old spends more than an hour a day with video games. The huge amount of time spent with video games during their formative years has led the G Generation to be "hard wired" differently than those who came before them.

Research done by The North Star Leadership Group led by John C. Beck, demonstrates that gamers show a range of different opinions and behaviors compared to their non-gamer co-workers.

For example, instead, of trying to seek "one" answer, games teach there are many potential paths to "victory," and one should try as many as possible to see what happens. Victory is possible – the game designer wouldn't have made the game without a way to win.

Gamers are more likely to believe that "winning is everything" and "competition is the law of nature" than non-gamers.

Gamers believe that the world is a competitive place, and standing still won't get you anywhere. If there's a fork in the road, take one and see what happens.

Finally, games teach that being the hero is important — people are counting on you to save the day and defeat the evil "level boss" … they've been taught their entire lives to dispatch with those in authority as quickly as possible (Carstens and Beck, 2005)

10,000 Hours to Become an Expert ... But at What?
By one estimate, typical American teens will have played
ten thousand hours of digital games by the time they begin
their careers. (Prensky, 2001)

In the book *Outliers*, Malcolm Gladwell puts forth the
premise that to be an expert in your field requires a devo-
tion to one's craft for at least 10,000 hours. Californian
game designer Jane McGonigal, says that a dedicated
gamer will spend 10,000 hours playing by the time they
turn 21 – the time it takes to become an "expert."

So the question is, just what exactly has the G Generation
become experts at? And how have these 10,000 hours af-
fected the way the G Generation views the business world?

Right now the G Generation is moving up in the business
ranks, becoming managers, partners, and eventually CEOs.
Chances are you manage employees from this generation,
and in all likelihood, before you leave your career, you may
be managed by them.

Gamers approach the business world more like a game.
They see the different companies—and maybe the people
they work with—as "players." They are competitive and
very passionate about "winning."

They are incredibly creative, optimistic, and determined
about solving any kind of problem you can imagine – be-
lieving there will always be some combination of moves
that will result in success.

They are very confident, and somewhat suspicious of
bosses or a company hierarchy – preferring to rely on their
own abilities to succeed or fail.

Gamers are comfortable with risks and they are resilient.
They know they can survive failure, because they have
failed thousands of times on the way to whatever "wins"

they have had within games.

The G Generation is more likely to believe that taking measured risks is the best way to get ahead. It's built into the way games are played ... if this doesn't work, I'll try it this way. If I'm stuck in a maze, I'll try this solution. In a game you are in a situation for a reason, and there is always a way to get out of it. All you have to do is find your way around it – or "solve" the problem.

Lessons Learned from Video Games
In the book, *The Kids Are All Right*, authors Beck and Wade go into depth in the lessons that the G Generation has learned from video games, after all, gamers spent substantial amounts of time sharpening their skills in a world that was created completely for them.

Generally, and almost subconsciously, games deliver a "reality" where the rules are quite different from those in the real world. Here is a quick overview of the lessons games teach:

> **You're the star.** You are the center of attention of every game, unlike, say, Little League, where most kids will never be the star.

> **You're the boss.** The world is very responsive to you. You can choose things about reality, or switch to different experiences, in a way that is literally impossible in real life.

> **There's always an answer.** You might be frustrated for a while, you might even never find it, but you know it's there.

> **Trial and error is almost always the best approach.** It's the only way to advance in most games, even if you break down and buy a strategy

guide or ask others how they got through the hard parts.

It's all about competition. You're always competing; even if you collaborate with other players, you're competing against some character or score.

Make your own way in the world. Leaders are irrelevant and often evil; ignore them.

Although these lessons are not exactly like real life, the G Generation has grown up in this game world.

The question is whether these lessons make a difference as they enter and begin to lead in the workplace. According to the research of Beck and Wade, it appears that these lessons will have a more positive effect than most people imagine.

The G Generation will change business because of who they are, how they grew up, how they see the world, and how they go after what they want.

The 7 Habits of Highly Typical Gamers.

1. **Everyone Can Succeed.** Gamers grew up in a world where everyone can succeed at just about anything. This gives them courage, ambition, and persistence. By working hard and long enough, it is possible for every player to win.

2. **You Gotta Play The Odds.** Gamers are twice as likely as Boomers to believe success in life is due to luck. This prepares them to regard failure as a learning experience in which their luck just ran out.

3. **Learn From The Team, Not The Coach.** Gamers love working together and helping each other – they learn by doing, together. Sometimes you can teach a point better by introducing a group of gamers to a problem and then just getting out of their way.

4. **Kill Bosses, Trust Strategy Guides.** In video games, the "level boss" is the toughest obstacle to get past to achieve your goal. As a result, they have some issues with authority. But, they love strategy guides — books and websites, written by a peer, with insider tips on how to win the game.

5. **Watch The Map.** Because video games can be complex, gamers rely on a grid that shows where they are in relation to other players, goals, obstacles, and resources. They know exactly where they are and what they need to win.

6. **Can't See It? Ignore It.** In video games the action is all on the surface, there are never any unseen enemies. This generation can become confused and angered when let down by unseen forces in organizations. They become frustrated by decisions from people they can't confront.

7. **Demand The Right Team.** In gaming, there's nothing more frustrating than playing with someone who doesn't "get it." Groups thrown together casually, because of institutional structure or a need for balance just don't work for them. Find teams that match their level — and their passion for a particular challenge — and you'll be amazed at what they can do.

(Beck and Wade, 2006)

Chapter 4—

Playing the Game

Gamification invites people to participate and engage by integrating game mechanics and game dynamics into such things as a website, online community, marketing campaign, or even a traditional training and development program. By adding game mechanics to training, Gamification not only increases interest, it makes training "fun."

The goal is to increase learning and engagement through key concepts found in game design and behavioral psychology. When participants first encounter the game, they rely upon a combination of visual cues, called game elements, to not only understand how the game is played, but also how success is defined and determined. The most common cues include:

- Points
- Badges
- Levels
- Rewards or Unlocks
- Collections
- Leaderboards
- Player Pieces or Avatars
- Maps and Game Boards
- Narrative or Instructions

Points
People love piling up points. They love to earn them, bank them, and make sure others know how many points they have. Usually participants can spend points to unlock access to content, or to "acquire" virtual goods, or to even gift their points to other participants. In short, people love to be rewarded even if there's no monetary value associated with

the reward.

Badges, Trophies, Achievements
Trophies, badges, ribbons, etc. are the visible recognition of having reached new levels or completed challenges. Challenges give people goals and the feeling that they're working toward something. Once a level or challenge is completed, participants expect some type of recognition for the milestone. As silly as it might seem, trophies and badges matter; they are visual markers of attainment.

One of the keys to making levels and challenges effective is providing a forum for users to show off their achievements, like a trophy case or user profile page that displays their badges. You can also display the various badges that a player has yet to collect or earn. The display of unearned badges helps create motivation to keep earning and achieving; to say it another way, it increases and sustains engagement.

Levels
Levels are an indication that you've reached a milestone or overcome a specific challenge. Once a gamer completes a level and moves to the next one, status is obtained among other participants. Levels are often defined as point thresholds. Think of it like frequent-flyer programs. Amassing points isn't enough; people also want to attain certain levels such as gold and platinum. They do enjoy certain privileges at that level, but more often they want others to know about the level they've reached. They enjoy having a different boarding line.

Rewards/Unlocks
Games typically give players a payoff, even if it's only the enjoyment of playing. It is important to realize that participants in a gamified training activity want some sort of payoff. In training and development, tangible rewards could be as simple as increased recognition or some other work-related perk such as flexible work hours. The best reward

systems combine reward types. It's also important to the players that the reward structure is clearly explained. Confused players quickly lose interest in the game.

Collections
In games, people often gather collections of items. These collections create a level of complexity in a game. Simple points, levels, and rewards are not enough. Gamers like the added challenge of completing collections. Think of baseball cards or porcelain figurines. Once someone begins assembling a collection, they want to complete it, until every item of the collection is acquired. Usually it is easy to get the initial pieces of a collection, but as the game progresses, it becomes more difficult to complete the collection.

Leaderboards
Leaderboards increase competition. When participants see where they stand in relation to their peers, they work extra hard to surpass them. Often bragging rights are a bigger reward than other types of motivators.

Player Pieces or Avatars
Pieces or avatars show that the person is a player and they are in the game. They give people an identity within the game. Players often develop intense loyalty to their avatars, working hard to make sure they represent their avatar well.

Maps or Game Boards
Maps act as a reference point for players. They can see where they are, where they've been, and where they need to go. A good map also shows participants where they are in relation to the other players.

Narrative or Instructions
Each challenge should ideally have its own narrative or description in order to build a more substantial environment for the player. In games, they are not simply playing, they are also participating in a story. They are part of a made-up and challenges have a purpose in the narrative.

Game Mechanics that Motivate Behaviors

Game mechanics are the rules and rewards that make games challenging, fun, and satisfying. The addition of game mechanics enlivens your training and development programs. Participants are not only eager to get involved, they will also work extra hard to complete the game.

Gamified activities satisfy basic human desires such as winning, competition, overcoming challenges, even working with others to preserve community status. Gamification can also motivate participants to work through different levels of training.

It's important to understand that clicking a button for a reward is not a game mechanic. Gamers don't want simple rewards; they want to accomplish something and then receive recognition that they have attained a certain level or status. Status and a sense of accomplishment is more important than easy gifts.

There must be a beginning and a mastery stage in a game. During the beginning, or induction stage, users learn about the game, understand how rewards are obtained, and the overall progression process. Initially, they have easy "wins" as they move through the first levels. You want to minimize frustration and early dropout rates by reducing confusion and providing quick, easy wins in the beginning. Remember, the participant wants to have fun while playing.

Measuring progression and level completion is also important. Make sure your participants understand how you measure the success of the training program so that they can work toward your goals for the game.

You want to connect your measurements to the goals and outcomes you are seeking from the training or activity. For innovation and brainstorming applications, you may not have a specific picture of what the outcome should look like, but be clear about how players and management will know when the outcome has been reached.

Most current applications of game mechanics to training rely on monetary or other extrinsic rewards and a competitive game structure, but some research suggests that these rewards have not been very successful:

- A recent Gallup survey found that only 29% of employees are engaged at work, with 52% identifying themselves as unengaged, and 19% as disengaged.

- As Daniel Pink argues in the book *Drive: The Surprising Truth about What Motivates Us*, intrinsic rewards are far better than extrinsic rewards when seeking to create higher levels of engagement and better results.

Remember, gaming has created an entirely different learning style, one that:

- Aggressively ignores any hint of formal instruction.

- Relies heavily on trial and error (after all, failure is nearly free; you just push "play again").

- Includes lots of learning from peers, but virtually none from authority figures.

- Is consumed in very small bits exactly when the learner wants it, which is usually just before the skill is needed.

You should consider applying different game mechanics to different types of work to drive different types of behaviors, for instance:

- In low-skilled, repetitive jobs, present workers with specific tasks to be completed, and reward them for completing those tasks. Workers will be motivated with social recognition within the workgroup.

- In knowledge work, such as project management or product design where the process or outcome may be unknown, provide the players with the goals, tools, rules, and space to play, but let them have flexibility with their actions.

Start building your own gamified processes to see how they work and test the design to see actually happens versus what you anticipated would happen. You can also interview your players so that you understand what they liked and didn't like.

And don't forget the fun! If users are having fun, they are more likely to stay engaged. And when they are engaged, they are more likely to achieve performance goals.

Chapter 5—

Game Psych!

When you begin to gamify activities to achieve business objectives, it helps to understand the psychology of gaming. After all, you want to create an engaging experience that motivates participants.

Like well-designed games, well-designed Gamification will:
- Encourage problem solving
- Promote teamwork
- Give players a sense of control
- Reward out-of-the-box thinking
- Reduce the fear of failure that inhibits innovative experimentation
- Support diverse interests and skill sets

How Are People Motivated By Game Mechanics?
We all desire reward, status, achievement, self-expression, competition, and altruism. These needs cross generations, demographics, cultures, and genders. Best of all, they are key to games.

Game designers know how to focus on these needs and desires, and now Gamification allows you to have that same focus. By designing the appropriate set of game mechanics into your gamified training programs, you can create an experience that drives behavior by fulfilling one or more of these needs:

> **Reward -** Who doesn't like a reward? Especially when it is given to us in recognition of a challenge we overcame. The primary reward within Gamifica-

tion is early points, much like a frequent flier program. And you can also give participants badges, trophies, virtual goods, even recognition when they move from one level to the next.

Status - Most of us have a need for status, recognition, fame, prestige, attention and, ultimately, the esteem and respect of others. Leveling-up (such as getting a gold or platinum credit card) is one of the primary motivators in Gamification. When you add Gamification to your training, make sure you include levels.

Achievement - Some of us are motivated by a need to accomplish something difficult. People motivated by achievement tend to seek out challenges, set moderately difficult goals, and receive satisfaction when they are recognized for their achievements.

Self-expression - Many people have a desire to exhibit a sense of style, identity, and personality. They may also want to flaunt an affiliation with a certain group. Using an avatar can serve as a powerful focal point for self expression. As they identify with their avatar, people begin to express their loyalty to the avatar by working extra hard to make sure it progresses in the game.

Competition - We gain a certain amount of satisfaction by comparing our performance to others. Higher levels of performance can be achieved when a competitive atmosphere is established and the winner rewarded. The use of leaderboards is essential to showing off. As participants move from level to level, make sure they get recognized and their achievement celebrated. A simple top-ten list can display new levels achieved, rewards earned, or challenges overcome. Not only will those on the list have pride in accomplishment, but others will also strive to be on the list.

Altruism - In a community where people seek to cultivate relationships, gift-giving is a strong motivator. In Gamification, gifting is an incredible mechanic. You receive a gift from someone to draw you into the game, you're incentivized to send gifts to all your friends, and every time you receive a gift, it draws you back in to redeem it. Not all gifts are equal, so motivated gifters will seek out more valuable forms of expression.

Types of Game Players
Richard Bartle is a British professor and game researcher, and is one of the pioneers of the massively multiplayer online game industry. Bartle did research on player personality types in massively-multiplayer online games, and his research was put into a test to classify players.

The Bartle Test of Gamer Psychology is a series of questions and an accompanying scoring formula that classifies players as an explorer, socializer, killer, or achiever. The result of the Bartle Test is known as the "Bartle Quotient." it calculates a person's classification based on the answers to a series of 30 random questions that total 200% across all categories, with no single category exceeding 100%.

For example, a person may score "100% Killer, 50% Socializer, 40% Achiever, 10% Explorer," which means the player prefers fighting other players compared to any other area of interest.

Scores are typically abbreviated by the first letter of each category, in order of the quotient. In the previous example, this result would be described as a "KSAE" result.

Although the test was originally designed for MUD (Multi-User Dungeon) participants, such as World of Warcraft,

Examples of Motivators Supported by Game Mechanics

Motivators	Possible Game Mechanics that Provide Support
Autonomy	Customization Choice Freedom
Mastery	Levels Challenges
Purpose	Giving or Altruism Narrative Greater Meaning
Status	Leaderboards Achievements
Social Connections	Suggest similar users Cooperative "play"
Rewards	Points Badges Achievements
Peer Pressure	Peer review, feedback, grading Boasting or Bragging system Competitive play
Avoidance	Lose Points Lose Status Game Over
Scarcity	Exclusive or Unique Rewards Reward Schedules
Fun!	Real Games Quiz's Competitions

(Marczewski, 2013)

Bartle believes that the test is relevant to Gamification players as well.

You can follow this link to take the original Bartle test to see what kind of gaming personality you are: http://www.gamerdna.com/quizzes/

An easy way to remember the four styles is to associate them with the suits in a standard deck of playing cards:

- Achievers are Diamonds – they're always seeking treasure.
- Explorers are Spades – they dig around for information.
- Socializers are Hearts - they empathize with the other players.
- Killers are Clubs – they hit people with clubs.

Players often move between the four styles, depending on their mood or the current game. However, most players have a primary style, and will only switch to other styles as a means to advance in the game.

Let's look at each player type in detail:

Achievers: Also known as "Diamonds," these players see gathering points, badges, levels, and other measurements of success in a game, as their main goal. They will go to great lengths to achieve rewards for prestige, even if the rewards have little application or notice outside of the game.

Achievers like the opportunity to show off their skills and hold elite status. They also like seeing their usernames at the top of leaderboards.

Achievers say things like:
- "I'm busy."
- "Sure, I'll help you. What do I get?"

- "Only 3412 points to go!"

Explorers: Explorers, called "Spades" for their tendency to dig around, discover new areas, and learn about hidden places. The real fun comes from discovering, and making complete sets of collections. They traditionally like games where the objective is to find your way out of a predicament by paying close attention to detail and solving puzzles.

Explorers don't like games that expect them to move on within a certain amount of time, because that does not allow them to look around. They find great joy in discovering an unknown glitch or a hidden charm.

However, Explorers will often become bored with any particular game once they feel it has become a chore to play, or when they believe nothing new lies ahead.

Explorers say things like:
- "Hmm..."
- "You mean you *don't know* the shortest route from (Obscure Point A) to (Obscure Point B)
- "I haven't tried that one, what's it do?"

Socializers: There are a multitude of gamers who play for the social aspect; they don't care about the game itself. These players are known as Socializers, or "Hearts." They gain the most enjoyment from interacting with other players. The game is merely a backdrop, a common ground where things happen.

Since their objective is not so much to win or explore, there are few games that the Socializers enjoy based on their own merits. Instead, Socializers use their experience to socialize with those who have played them.

Socializers say things like:
- "Hi!"
- "Really? Oh no! Gosh, that's awful! Are you sure?"
- "What happened? I missed it. I was talking."

Killers: "Clubs" is a perfect nickname for what the Killer likes to do ... club people. They thrive on competition with other players. They're in it for the sport, trying to read their opponent's moves.

Some Killers are actually nice people who thrive on competition. But for some, it's more about power and the ability to "hurt" others. Their natural drive to compete stirs up trouble.

Killers says things like:
- "Ha!"
- "Coward!"
- "Die!"

(Killers are people of few words.)

Competition vs. Collaboration
Games are, by definition, competitive, whether you're competing against yourself, other players, or the game itself.

Competition within your gamified training and development programs is beneficial because it motivates players to higher levels of engagement and encourages teammates to motivate each other. Losing a game can lead to greater learning as long as there is reflection and critical thinking, instead of just frustration. Plus, players can learn good sportsmanship skills from winning and losing.

However, in today's workplace, competition might not be good because it can increase hostility between co-workers, weaken the intrinsic motivation to learn the content because of the focus on winning, and can reduce confidence levels and lead to lower self-esteem

On the other hand, collaboration is considered a good skill for employees to learn and put into practice. Some of the benefits of collaboration include fostering teamwork and other social skills, creating a greater sense of purpose by being part of something bigger, and it provides a motivation to help your group succeed.

Most of the time, you want to design a game to have enough competition to motivate, but not so much that it detracts from learning collaborative skills. If you put too much emphasis on competition, the focus is on winning and not on helping others. On the other hand, if you put too much emphasis on collaboration, you run the risk of turning a fun motivating game into a boring team-building activity.

For example, say there is a three-person team strategic thinking game where each team has an hour to design a new supply-chain distribution route. If the emphasis is on competition (winning), it's likely that one person does everything and no collaboration takes place. But, if the main emphasis is on collaboration where every person must be assigned to one of three tasks, then the game may start to feel like a group-work assignment, not a game.

Ideally, you should design games that use competition to improve collaborative skills. For example:

- In charades or Guesstures, in order to win, partners have to learn to collaborate better to understand each person's non-verbal communication patterns.

- In basketball, the desire to win forces players to collaborate — passing the ball to the teammate rather than going for the glory of the 3-point shot.

- In the video game Rockband, competition spurs collaboration to get a higher score if you and your friends aspire to be the best rock band in the world.

So, when you are designing or evaluating a gamified learning process, make sure you take some time to reflect on the balance and interdependency of the competitive and collaborative elements in the game. These elements could very well be the key to the game's ability to engage, motivate, and educate players.

Wherever there are employees, there are people to be motivated.

- Salespeople can be incentivized to increase revenues and focus on desired product mixes by the use of competition and challenges
- Customer-support personnel can be motivated to offer better service through the use of a customer feedback system
- All employees can be motivated to take part in optional training programs that will boost their careers and make them more valuable to the company

Gamification can be applied across a broad spectrum of situations in your workplace, where individuals need to be motivated or incentivized to take part in specific actions or activities to achieve business objectives.

Chapter 6—

Think Like a Gamer

Gamification does **NOT** equal technology ... it is really a way of thinking about the development and delivery of your training programs.

Gamification can play a key role in how your organization trains employees when you learn how to think like a game designer.

Gamification forces directors of training and development within organizations to think through how to make learning more engaging. Creating a game can be a complex, time consuming and difficult process; however, adding game elements to your training and development programs is less complicated than you think.

When developing learning experiences, if you think like a game-designer, you will provide a more realistic and rich approach to all types of training. The ultimate result of thinking like a game designer is that the training programs that are developed will be more engaging and motivating for the learner.

Of course, Gamification can be costly, and that cost may be considered a barrier by some. When most people think of games and simulations, they think of high costs and the large time commitment of development, testing, and implementation.

However, Gamification can be done at a reduced cost and within the same relative time frame as the development of traditional instruction. Additionally, it doesn't need to be focused only on online games or internet-based or mobile applications.

There are four elements that are contained in games that you can use them to gamify most training experiences:
1. Challenge
2. Interaction
3. Storyline
4. Feedback

All good games begin with a challenge, so instead of thinking about creating learning objectives, Gamification allows you to think about creating a challenge.

Similarly, all good games contain interaction. Gamification is not about lists of bulleted instruction; instead, it is about interaction.

Good games are framed around a compelling story. What do you remember from a training or workshop experience that you have participated in? Facts, figures, and statistics? Not likely. It's the stories. We learn best from the analogies and remember the stories. Gamification allows you to design your training around a story.

Finally, most games provide continual, focused feedback. Gamification of your training using points, badges, levels, and leaderboards provides these elements of continual feedback about progress and advancement.

Adding these elements to instruction provides engagement, a context where learning takes place, and gives participants a chance to apply the learning. All of these are elements from games that can be incorporated into training.

Examples of Low Tech Gamification
Let me give you two examples of projects I've been involved in recently to illustrate my point about not needing technology for Gamification projects. Both examples in-

volve training that is considered complex and perhaps a little dull. By using basic Gamification techniques, the participants not only learned the material, but were completely engaged and having fun throughout the program.

Snow White's Payroll Administration

The first example of low-tech Gamification involves a workshop on Payroll Administration. I was hired by a company to deliver payroll administration training at 20 sites across the country for their current and perspective clients.

The course was designed in a very traditional fashion, starting with several course objectives such as, "The learner will understand how to ensure you're withholding, reporting, and paying the right taxes." Then the course provided a list of terminologies participants had to learn, plus an alphabet soup of local, state and federal acronyms. The problem was that after the individuals left the six-hour class, they still felt uneasy and uncertain about whether they were complying with payroll laws.

I decided to mix it up a little and add Gamification to the instruction. (The lawyer who designed the course was not happy or excited about this at all!)

The class opened with me holding an apple in my hand and saying the following, "What does an apple have to do with payroll administration?" Of course I was met with uncertain looks. I then said, "What if I told you this was a poison apple? What could the poison apple represent? Could it be not knowing the facts, violating the laws, getting caught, and even being forced to submit to a Department of Labor or IRS audit? That's why we're here today – so you don't ever have to take a bite of the poison apple."

The rest of the day was centered on a spinoff of the traditional story of *Snow White and the Seven Dwarfs*. Each of the characters were developed to be included in the problems, calculations, and assessments. For example:

> **Grumpy:** No matter what anyone says, Grumpy is against it. He's a know-it-all naysayer with the personality of an old boot. But, why do think he's Grumpy? Could it be because he has an ex-wife, and hasn't paid child support, and now his wages are being garnished? It's no wonder he's Grumpy!

> **Dopey:** Well, he's the boss's son. We're not sure what he does. His job description has him classified as an Executive Exempt – but you're not sure he qualifies.

Throughout the day, there were individual and team activities, competitions, quizzes and "test your knowledge" checkpoints. All were based on the storyline and included many elements of just plain fun, like trying to apply the IRS guidelines to determine if the Woodsman was an independent contractor or an employee of the Queen.

The last challenge of the day was a recap of the key points via a case study. When the participants were able to make recommendations that were in line with payroll guidelines, they received gems to glue onto their crown. Seems rather childish? I had the entire "C" team of the organization battling to get the correct recommendations and earn the most jewels. It was fascinating and rewarding to watch how simply adding challenge, interaction, a storyline, and feedback to an otherwise "dry" topic created an engaged and enthusiastic room of learners.

The Riddle of the Exporter™
The second example comes from a colleague who developed a two-day export training program called The Riddle of the Exporter™. (www.riddleoftheexporter.com)

Exporting is an extremely complex topic, and The Riddle

of the Exporter™ creates an eight-step process that serves as a roadmap for new exporters. The training gives an overview of exporting, provides participants with a process to use, and then shows them how to use the process by walking through an export transaction ... all while being entertained!

Instructional designer and creator of the program, Elyse Eriksson believes there are three components to a good game: knowledge, skill, and luck. If you think about it, it's the same with life. The Riddle of the Exporter™ training/ game is modeled on these three components.

The entire training is a game or puzzle from beginning to end. The training starts with an actual Riddle of the Exporter (http://www.youtube.com/watch?v=Ouq6z4leah0) made up of numerous acronyms and exporting jargon. This lets the participants see how much they don't know!

The game's storyline is centered on imaginary characters, Ernie Earl and Betty Sue from Gun Barrel City, Texas. (The point being that if Ernie Earl and Betty Sue can export ... anyone can export.) The four teams help Ernie Earl and Betty Sue export four products to four different countries to determine "Who Wants to be an Export Millionaire?"

At the end of each of the eight steps, there is a simple test that earns the teams points in a variety of ways, there is also a skill activity that varies with each step, and finally "Good Luck/Bad Luck Cards" because even if you do everything right in life, some things still rely on simply being lucky.

Scattered throughout are some big bonus points. If they ask the instructor a question she tells them to get on the Internet and look up the answer. They get big points for this. Some people spend their break time looking up things on the Internet!

At the end of Day Two, each team must present a launch

plan for their product using the eight-step process. Because, the game concept allows them to loosen up and have fun, participants get amazingly creative with the presentation. This combined with points determines the winning team.

What do they "win"? A trophy of course – a really tacky, gold, plastic cowboy boot with a globe on top. Each member of the team gets a yellow cowboy rubber ducky. In the end, Betty Sue makes a guest appearance. People love her!

The training ends with the same Riddle and this time the entire audience knows the acronyms, demonstrating how much they have learned. Attendees are amazed that this complex topic can be understood in two days. For some, the goal is to pass the SBA Export Trade and Counseling Certification and participants of this training have a 99% pass rate.

All throughout the two-day class, participants are guided by the instructor. This immerses them in the learning process, and at the end of the two days they have actually conducted a mock exporting of a product. They know what forms to use, what questions to ask, and what procedures to follow. They know because they did it.

That is an example of a simulation that doesn't require high -tech programming or development. What it requires is thinking like a game developer. It requires elements of Gamification to take typical training delivery, and transform it into an engaging experience for the learners.

Aligning the Game with Your Goal
The focus is the Gamification of training to help participants improve their understanding of their organizations or business processes. The games may also be designed to help participants observe and change their own behaviors, develop better team skills, and improve their ability to manage problems.

The game should never be seen as an end in itself or positioned to be able to deliver value all by itself. It should be secondary to clearly defined learning objectives.

To be effective, the goals, activities, and feedback must align with the desired instructional outcomes. There are many different game types (action-adventure, role play, strategy, etc.) and it is important that the game-type aligns with the learning goal.

> **Goals:** A single, clearly defined overall goal is important. To design a game you begin with the end in mind – you need to know the goal of the game. What do you want to have accomplished by the end of the game? What does victory look like? What's the take away?
>
> The game should be based around real business issues, dilemmas, or trade-offs, and not right or wrong answers. The right issues will inspire rich conversations and give players the opportunity to learn from each other. The most useful games focus on specific company "pain-points" rather than just generic business challenges.
>
> **Activities:** Good games are not too easy, but not too hard either. In order to manage complexity, our games should move from simple to complex, the difficulty has to match the participants' abilities, so they are properly challenged.
>
> This is a fine balance. A game, which is too easy, allows participants to be distracted by other things; and it it's too hard, they get frustrated. The game has to strike the right balance, and keep getting more difficult as they improve their skills.
>
> It is particularly important for participants not to ex-

perience frustration, but instead reach some measurement of success shortly after starting the game the first time. You have to capture their interest immediately – put a smile on their face within a few minutes. Provide a tutorial if necessary to explain what the game is about, but keep it concise and easy-to-understand.

Feedback: Feedback mechanisms are also vital. Participants need to constantly be told whether they are getting closer to or further away from their goal. Positive reinforcement is a great motivator. Getting praise makes us happy, boosts our confidence, and pushes our efforts further.

Giving out scores is one of the oldest and most widely used techniques. Points, badges, levels, and leaderboards can be used to track progress and to maintain a picture of the game's current state. This keeps the audience motivated.

Bragging rights can be a big motivating factor, making some kind of feedback or scoring systems – including achievements – a valuable asset to your game.

When participants enter into a gamified learning environment, the rules of ordinary life are temporarily suspended and replaced with the rules of the game. To enter a game space, the players must agree to abide by the rules of that space and know when the game is over – an end state that they are all striving to attain. Most important, they must enter willingly. It's not a game if people are forced to play.

It's very important to build in some elements of novelty and lightness. Overly serious games bring little enjoyment. However, playfulness and fun are both great catalysts for learning.

Chapter 7—

Game Over?

When designed correctly, Gamification has proven to be very successful in engaging people and motivating them to change behaviors, develop skills, or solve problems. Leveraging some of the features used in real games, Gamification can turn many other types of activities into games.

But like most things, simply tacking on Gamification to a shoddy process or ambiguous objectives is poor execution and will lead to poor results.

Gartner Research Company predicts that by 2014, 80 percent of current gamified applications will fail to meet business objectives, primarily due to poor design. The design flaws will be in the area of defining business objectives and implementation.

The ultimate goal in Gamification is to provide a layer of motivation. The feedback of points, badges, and levels inherently creates competition among its users.

From a business perspective, this makes a lot of sense. However, there are some pitfalls of Gamification. Yet, if a company gets it right, they can motivate their employees to become more engaged, productive, and invested, which will help to achieve performance goals and business objectives. Reducing gaming to its reward systems is like missing out on the actual race and skipping to the medal ceremony. Points and badges are game elements, but they are not the game.

While extrinsic rewards motivate behavior – would you go to your job every day if you didn't get paid – research suggests that when we're paid to do something you would usually consider play, you soon start seeing that thing as work.

Gamer Beware

We've discussed the framework and benefits of Gamification, but it's not a universal solution. There are several caveats that come with implementing a "gamified" training and development program. Shallow Gamification can lead to shallow engagement and low ROI. When rewards happen, how they happen, and how they aggregate are elements that need to be carefully considered and well integrated into the existing employee on-boarding, engagement, and training programs. Beware of:

> **Superficial Motivation** – Programs such as frequent flyer miles provide some real world incentive for activity and progress and provide tangible benefits. Adding game mechanics to your program will not automatically produce the same type of powerful engagement and behavior changing results. Slapping points, badges, and leaderboards into your training may result in the motivation being contained within the game and not attached to the outcomes you are trying to create.

> **Ranking Becomes Trivial** - Sometimes the method of reaching the highest rank can become trivial when the only important aspect of the game is reaching that spot. The user is targeting their motivation towards being the best and not at seeing what the training program has to offer. This may seem irrelevant if an employee is still spending time on the requisite activity. However, it's also not building true engagement or reaching performance goals.

> **Poor Implementation** - Poor Gamification implementation may remove a lot of the fundamental

nature or spirit of games. It can become almost a cut-and-paste process that lacks originality or creativity. Traditional games are about discovery and overcoming trials, and you want to be sure to keep those game mechanics in your gamified solutions.

Time to Design - The Gamification technology companies (See Gamification Sources Chapter) make it seem easy to attach Gamification to your training and development program. But to reach its true potential the gamified elements need to be well designed and thought out. This should take a fairly significant amount of time to get right.

To achieve the most success, consider the following points before jumping unprepared into the Gamification crowd.

Clearly Identify the Performance Goals or Business Objectives – Instead of asking, "How can we leverage Gamification in our organization?" begin with clearly defined business objectives and a critical analysis of the suitability of Gamification to achieve those business objectives.

Do Not Confuse Activity with Success – You will hear how leading-edge companies leverage Gamification, but you don't necessarily hear about the quantified results they have achieved. Rather than narratives that simply describe what has been done, look for examples of companies in your industry that have used Gamification to help them achieve their business objectives.

Think of the Audience as Players not Puppets – Slapping some meaningless points, badges, and leaderboards into your training and development program does not mean that you will now be able to get employees to readily do what they have been unwilling or unable to do before. You must engage the target audience with meaningful incentives.

Design for Player-Centricity – The mistake many companies make is to identify the business objectives without clearly identifying the player objectives. The sweet spot for Gamification is where the business objectives and player objectives overlap. Gamified applications must be designed to motivate players to achieve their goals.

Companies and brands have long tried to attract attention and foster customer loyalty with special offers, free gifts, and competition give-aways, all of which have been short-term activities with short-term benefits.

To be truly effective, Gamification needs to use quality game design, not just points, badges, trophies, and levels. No amount of leveling up or extrinsic reward can replace the engagement created by an actual game.

Chapter 8—

Reboot

While points, badges, and leaderboards are important elements of Gamification projects, Gamification is more than just pouring these elements onto a business process like hot fudge on chocolate chip cookie dough ice cream. Gamification requires a great deal of thought about the entire design of the system, including understanding the nature of your users, thinking about what you'd like them to do, and how best to make them do it.

You must consider whether to use no tech or to add technology, the best technology platform to use, and examine the specific game elements and game mechanics you're going to incorporate. In this guide, we've learned some very specific lessons about how to implement Gamification design, and how to add in levers of motivation and behavior modification that work.

It's likely we'll start to see internal Gamification in many more business sectors, and that it will become more important in training and development programs. Imaginative executives will build it into areas that we haven't seen before and use it to increase productivity in almost all parts of business. We'll probably see this happen first in human resources and sales, where motivating staff is already a well-known process in need of repair.

The future of Gamification is not predictable, but it will become more commonplace in the next few years. In time, the hype will die down, replaced by the recognition that Gamification can deliver results as long as the design is properly thought through. Gamification will work and will become another tool in the modern manager's supervisory toolbox. Eventually, Gamification will be important to every part of business, even if it doesn't transform all of them.

If nothing else, it may make business and learning more fun!

Gamification works best when an initial effort focuses on implementing only one or a small handful of game elements into an environment or activity. For example, adding a simple progress bar, or awarding badges for engaging in or accomplishing straightforward activities, are great starting points. The important part of any initial venture into Gamification is to learn as one goes, weaving in increasingly complex elements and mechanics as competence and capabilities grow.

A critical part of good Gamification is to test or pilot the gamified environment. Testing helps answer a number of critical questions such as … is it fun, do your employees want to engage with this game, and will it result in the desired business outcomes?

Gamification, when used and designed properly, can prove enormously beneficial for companies. As with any fad, when it's used clumsily and hastily it begins to lose its value and gain criticism. The elements that make it so powerful are not trivial or plug-and-play features.

As with any type of educational design, it needs to be carefully considered, designed, and reviewed. If we're going to gamify our training and development, then we need to have knowledge of game design and understand the potential pitfalls.

Gamification can increase motivation and engagement in users, but to get there we need to examine our own programs and processes in the context of Gamification instead of considering Gamification as simply a supplementary feature.

Regardless of what the future holds, the ability to shape and leverage Gamification as a powerful mechanism for motivating individuals and driving behavior rests in the hands of those who begin to use it today.

Take the first step. Use a progress bar, avatar, challenge, or reward, and you will start on an adventure that will benefit you and your organization.

Chapter 9—

Gamification Sources

Gamification is changing the way corporations, non-profits, brands, human resources, and training and development leaders engage and relate to their customers and employees, and the demand for Gamification products and services is growing rapidly

By 2015, Gartner Group projects that over 70% of the world's largest companies will be using Gamification.

There are a myriad of Gamification platforms you can choose from to help you implement a Gamification strategy. The tracking of achievements of all players and the implementation of rules and goals will be administered through the platform and so it is an essential piece for the success of a corporate or enterprise Gamification strategy.

Depending on the focus of your Gamification strategy, some platforms and business models will be a better fit.

42 Terabytes
A boutique content and strategy firm specializing in social rewards platforms and gamification initiatives.
http://42Terabytes.com

500friends
is dedicated to helping retailers increase lifetime value by maximizing the profitability of their customer relationships.
www.500friends.com

Badgeville
Founded in 2010 to revolutionize the analytics industry and

bring modern engagement experiences to every web and mobile property, Badgeville draws on proven techniques from social gaming, traditional loyalty programs and social networking in its acclaimed suite of Behavior Lifecycle Management solutions.
www.badgeville.com

Bennu
Combines gamification and social media marketing to make sustainability fun and profitable.
www.bennuworld.com

BigDoor
A full service platform that provides web publishers with an easy to implement, customizable loyalty program designed to acquire new users as well as engage and reward existing audiences.
http://BigDoor.com

Bunchball
The industry leader in gamification. Companies use Bunchball's Nitro gamification platform, and its powerful analytics solution, to create customized, actionable and scalable user experiences for consumers, employees and partners.
www.bunchball.com

Dopamine
A creative agency focused on fun, innovative, gamified campaigns for employees and consumers. Dopamine is headed by one of the world's foremost gamification experts, Gabe Zichermann. http://dopa.mn

eMee
A comprehensive social gamification platform enabling engagements in an online world with the aim to bring a revolutionary change in the employee engagement and social collaboration aspects of HR organizations.
http://www.eMee.co.in

ExpertOffice

An enterprise question-and-answer platform. Employees can ask questions on ExpertOffice and collaborate to find the best solution. Points are awarded to the employee that answered the question correctly making a fun and rewarding experience that promotes knowledge sharing.
http://www.expertoffice.com

Game Craft

A Bulgarian creative agency in the field of game design and gamification offers tailor made consulting for integrating gamification in products or projects at every stage of growth.
http://game-craft.com

Gigya

Provides websites with a complete social infrastructure that creates immersive social experiences for users and provides unparalleled customer insights for businesses.
www.gigya.com

Growth Engineering

Creates compelling eLearning content, provides a learning platform that is easy and fun to use, and offers full social-media integration.
http://www.growthengineering.co.uk/

Healthper

Combines a healthy gaming and social networking to create a fun and engaging experience to change behavior. Members are able to choose their games, which are designed to achieve personal goals, thus paving the way to a healthier lifestyle.
http://healthper.com

Hoopla

A leader in performance optimization for front line employees including sales, call centers, and support organizations. Allows users to define, track, and broadcast key metrics

and milestones and create and manage games and contests.
http://www.hoopla.net/

Hopskoch
Allows users to collaboratively author, distribute and measure the effectiveness of gamified interactive marketing across your channels.
http://hopskoch.com

IActionable
Focuses on driving improved employee behavior with gamification modules targeted to specific issues such as training, adoption, compliance and productivity.
www.iactionable.com

INXPO
INXPO's software enables organizations to create online destinations where communities interact live, and content is consumed and acted upon. Their web-based environments are based on three products: Webcasting, Online Events and Social Business TV, and are used for marketing, HR, internal communications, and training.
www.inxpo.com

Leaderboarded
A web app to create an engaging leaderboard that collects player points from multiple sources. Share the leaderboard as a themed web page or embed it as a widget on your existing site.
http://www.leaderboarded.com

LevelEleven
Develops easy-to-use software tools that help sales and other managers keep their teams focused on the right things. Our flagship product, Contest Builder, is a salesforce.com app that gives companies new ways to motivate key sales activities, call center response times, and general adoption.
http://leveleleven.com

Mindspace
Uses a consultative, strategic approach to harness the power of games for the benefit of clients.
http://www.mindspace.net

Morsekode
A creative agency with a focus on modern media that creates measurable engagement for clients by generating unique ideas and producing online and offline branded experiences, often in the form of gamification strategies, websites, mobile apps and custom video content.
www.morsekode.com

Mozilla Open Badge Network
Using Mozilla's Open Badge Infrastructure, any organization or community can issue badges backed by their own seal of approval. Learners and badge earners can then collect badges from different sources and display them across the web—on their resume, web site, social networking profiles, job sites or just about anywhere.
www.openbadges.org

PlayGen
Work at the crossroads of meaningful play, behavioral economics, social interaction and game design.
www.playgen.com

Playbasis
Gives brands, publishers, and merchants the ability to add fun, interactivity, and engagement to their products and services.
http://www.playbasis.com

PlayVoxa
A social colaboration platform designed to manage and motivate people in Contact Centers.
http://playvox.com

PunchTab
An engagement and incentives platform, powering loyalty programs, giveaways and customized campaigns for agencies, brands & bloggers.
http://www.punchtab.com

There are many more companies than the ones that I have listed here, and new platforms are being added to the mix regularly. In addition you can find numerous books, blogs, whitepapers, and wikis that will assist you in your entry into the world of Gamification.

Even with the plethora of game mechanics available that you can use to increase employee and consumer engagement, it's important to remember that Gamification will only deliver results if implemented correctly. This means ensuring that Gamification complements your current strategy, and can be maintained in the long term to truly assist you in reaching your performance goals and business objectives.

"The core content experience needs to be good, compelling and meaningful. And as long as that is there, these tools drive actions around the content."
– Rajat Paharias, Founder of Bunchball

Bibliography

Arvizu, Shannon, *6 Basic Principles for Learning Game Design,* 2012 http://www.shannonarvizu.com/2012/04/17/6-basic-principles-for-learning-game-design/

Beck, John C., and Wade, Mitchell, *The Kids are Alright.* Harvard Business School Publishing, 2006.

Burke, Brian, *The Gamification of Business,* Gartner, Inc http://www.forbes.com/sites/gartnergroup/2013/01/21/the-gamification-of-business/

Burke, Brian, *Gamification 2020: What Is the Future of Gamification?.* Gartner, Inc., 2012, http://www.gartner.com/technology/research/gamification/

Carstens and Beck, *Get Ready for the Gamer Generation.* TechTrends, 2005, http://johncbeck.com/gotgamebook/Get%20Ready%20For%20The%20Gamer%20Generation.pdf

Chapman, Patrick, *Gamification and Game Mechanics Made Simple.* Nordic Press, NY Kindle Edition, 2012.

Emrich, Alan, *The Gamer Generation And Why Baby Boomers Shouldn't Worry so Much about Them,* http://www.alanemrich.com/SGI/Week_10/SGI%2010%20GAMER%20GENERATION.pdf

Gallup Employee Engagement Index http://www.gallup.com/poll/150383/Majority-American-Workers-Not-Engaged-Jobs.aspx

Gladwell, Malcolm, Outliers: The Story of Success. Little, Brown and Company, 2008.

Gray, Dave, Brown, Sunni, and Macunofo, James, *Gamestorming*. O'Reilly Media, Inc., 2010.

Kapp, Karl, Gamification in the Realm of Employee Training, Games, 2012, http://www.uleduneering.com/kappnotes/index.php/2012/08/gamification-in-the-realm-of-employee-training/

Marczewski, Andrzej, *Game Mechanics in Gamification*. Tech & Gadgets, 2013, http://marczewski.me.uk/

McGonigal Jane, *Gaming can Make a Better World*. Ted Talk, 2010, http://www.ted.com/talks/jane_mcgonigal_gaming_can_make_a_better_world.html

Mellor, Louisa, *How Gamification is Changing the Web* http://www.louisamellor.com/?p=425

Pink, Daniel H., *Drive: The Surprising Truth About What Motivates Us*. Riverhead Press, 2009

Prensky, Marc, *Digital Game-Based Learning*. New York: McGraw Hill, 2001.

Smith, Justin, *The Benefits and Pitfalls of Gamification*. 2012, http://webdesign.tutsplus.com/articles/general/the-benefits-and-pitfalls-of-gamification/

Whitepaper, *5 Key Engagement Imperatives* www.badgeville.com

Whitepaper, *Gamification 101*. www.bunchball.com/gamification101

Werbach, Kevin; Hunter, Dan, *For the Win: How Game Thinking Can Revolutionize Your Business.* Wharton Digital Press, Kindle Edition, 2012.

Zichermann, Gabe and Linder, Joselin, *Game-Based Marketing: Inspire Customer Loyalty Through Rewards, Challenges, and Contests.* John Wiley and Sons, 2010.

Hire Monica to Speak

Do you feel that your organization is capable of higher productivity? Are you looking for a tangible way to boost staff morale? Is it time to get more from your customer engagement or training and development programs?

When it comes to choosing a dynamic, motivational speaker for your next event, you'll find no one more qualified or gifted than Monica Cornetti. Featured on the cover of Bloomberg's Businessweek, she is considered one of the leading authorities on entrepreneurial thinking and leadership in the business.

Monica is a highly sought after international keynote speaker and trainer. Her emphasis is always on **fun** as she delivers high-energy, high-content sessions, along with a plan for application in the real world.

With over 150 national, regional, and local speaking engagements each year, her keynotes are guaranteed to make you laugh ... make you cry ... and in the end provide your audience with information and motivation to create real change in their personal and professional lives!

If you are looking for an unforgettable speaker who will leave your audience wanting more, then book Monica Cornetti today.

Please email monica@monicacornetti.com, or call (972-951-3314) and Monica or one of her booking agents will get in touch with you to book your event and schedule a pre-speech interview.

Go to www.monicacornetti.com for demo videos and a complete list of topics.

Gamification 101:
Is Your Organization Ready for the Gamers

Program Length: Keynote or Breakout Session

Program Description:
This session is your opportunity to experience how Gamification can transform your organization and serve your customers and employees. Utilizing social media, mobile devices and gaming models, you'll examine case studies and be fully engaged in easy-to-implement games throughout the course.

Program Goals:
Understanding how and why gamification works, in what context it is most effective, and what the limits are to this approach of employee and client engagement will be highly useful for you and your staff. You will learn how to:
- Tackle your client engagement challenges with games
- Upgrade your organization's training and development through gaming scenarios
- Increase employee and client engagement from Millenials and Y Generations through game thinking
- Jump-start new clients into the culture of your organization
- Inspire positive interactions and increase economic impact

Program Outcome:
Participants in this innovative session will deepen their understanding of the five pillars of this cutting edge approach. By learning the theory and practice of Gamification, you organization can position itself to apply game mechanics in a manner that engages both internal and external stakeholders.

Enough already!
No more dry, boring lectures!

Whether you are a seasoned trainer or have never conducted training before, you can learn how to deliver totally awesome training sessions that will keep your participants coming back for more!

This 60-Minute Audio CD is specifically designed for individuals and organizations who specialize in training small business owners and entrepreneurs.

This innovative program will help you to quickly and easily learn how to liven up your training programs so that you can become a more dynamic trainer. These methods increase participation, engage your audience, and get genuine results.

In this program you'll learn the awesome techniques to:
- Quickly establish rapport with your training participants
- Identify easy and effective ways to build credibility
- Position your point and grab your audience's attention
- Illuminate the ideas and skills you are presenting
- Choose learning activities that are meaningful to participants

Order this CD online at www.entreprenowonline.com

About the Author

Featured on the cover of Bloomberg Businessweek, Monica Cornetti has been designated as "one of the best" entrepreneurial training experts. She works with individuals and organizations who want to learn how to think differently to achieve different results.

Monica is a highly sought-after speaker because of her spunkiness and emphasis on fun while learning. She is the author of the forthcoming book What Were You Thinking?, and the acclaimed book Your Face Isn't Finished Until Your Lipstick Is On: Rules of the Women's Success Game.

Monica's client list includes: The Association of Small Business Development Centers, Texas Tech, Shell Oil, Infinisource, Proctor & Gamble, The Nature Conservancy, American Fidelity, FM Global, American Society of Women Accountants, The Society for Human Resource Management, Las Vegas Chamber of Commerce, MEED Center, International Association of Administrative Professionals, HR Southwest, City of Price, Utah, Greater El Paso Credit Union, and Severn Savings Bank.

Monica is a graduate of Seton Hill with a BA in psychology, and The University of Houston-Victoria where she earned a Masters Degree in Economic Development and Entrepreneurship, chosen by Forbes Small Business as one of the top online programs for Entrepreneurship in the nation.

Her audiences from Guam to Georgia and Maui to Maine give her Perfect 10 reviews!
.
Contact Information:
Monica Cornetti
monica@entreprenowonline.com

www.entreprenowonline.com

CPSIA information can be obtained at www.ICGtesting.com
Printed in the USA
LVOW10s1318090614

389234LV00011B/68/P